I0014827

EXCEL

2023

**A Comprehensive Guide to become an Expert
on Excel 2023 With All-in-One Approach**

Leonardo L. Wright

© Copyright 2023 by Leonardo Lomonaco- All rights reserved.

This paper is oriented to provide accurate and reliable information regarding the subject and matter covered. The publication is sold with the understanding that the publisher is not required to render accounting, officially licensed, or otherwise qualified services. If advice is needed, legal or professional advice should be sought from a person experienced in the profession. - From a statement of principles, which has been accepted and approved equally by a committee of the American Bar Association and a committee of publishers and associations. In no way is it legal to reproduce, duplicate, or transmit any part of this document either by electronic means or in printed form. Recording of this publication is strictly prohibited, and any storage of this document is not permitted except with the written permission of the publisher. All rights reserved. The information provided herein is stated to be true and consistent, in that any liability, in terms of carelessness or otherwise, from any use or misuse of any policy, process or direction contained within is the sole and total responsibility of the receiving reader. Under no circumstances shall any legal liability or fault be held against the publisher for any redress, damage, or monetary loss due to the information contained herein, either directly or indirectly. The respective authors own all copyrights not held by the publisher. The information contained herein is offered for informational purposes only and is universal as such. The presentation of the information is without contract or any kind of assurance of warranty. Trademarks used are without consent, and publication of the trademark is without permission or endorsement from the trademark owner. All trademarks and brands within this book are for clarification purposes only and are the property of the owners themselves, not affiliated with this document.

Excel Basic Level

Introduction

You may be amazed to know this, but the most popular software in offices around the world is a simple table. A table that is made of horizontal and vertical lines, like the grid of a crossword puzzle, but unlike the latter it has no black boxes and within it both letters and numbers can dwell.

The vertical lines are called columns while the horizontal ones are called rows; at the point where rows and columns intersect, cells are formed that are nothing more than simple containers of data-letters, numbers or results of operations-that give meaning to our using this program. In short, in one name Excel.

This table is more technically referred to as a spreadsheet or, as the Americans say spreadsheet, and it allows us to report quantities of data that we can add or subtract or even extrapolate to be able to create graphs capable of simplifying the view, as well as the interpretation, of a budget at a glance.

But has Excel always been used? Obviously not, as the history of computing shows, Excel was the latest evolution of a series of programs that originated well before with the intent of covering certain job requirements. The first was VICalc, which saw the light of day in the spring of 1979 thanks to two friends-Dan Brickman and Bob Frankston. The software was not only a success but dominated the market for a few years until the release of Lotus 123 in August 1981.

Lotus allowed it to run on much more powerful computers such as IBM Personal Computers, was easy to use and, like all things easy and straightforward, was an extraordinary success that allowed it to last a long time. For those days it also had another advantage: it worked in the textual environment (i.e., devoid of the modern graphical interfaces we are used to today) typical of machines based, for example, on the MS-DOS operating si theme.

From Lotus on, market demand for this type of software grew interestingly enough to arouse the attention of Microsoft itself, which, in 1985, gave birth to Excel. Little curiosity: Excel was born to run on Macintosh machines that were structurally different from the PC, instead of working by means of characters alone they presented everything by images. Therefore, Excel was offered on PCs only when the first version of Windows became available.

From here on, the pairing of Word and Excel, had a strong and continuous growth so much so that they became real standards in their market sector, as well as being, even today, the most popular software in their field.

A small note: The version of Excel used in writing this book is the 2019 version.

1. Create a new spreadsheet and save it in the different formats

As we saw in our Introduction, the worksheet is divided into cells, which turn out to be the intersection of the rows (numbered on the left) and columns of the sheet identified at the top with one or more letters of the alphabet.

BUT how large is an Excel sheet? A simple multiplication can tell us; we need only know that a single worksheet results in 1,048,576 rows and 16,384 columns. Their product then tells us that a single sheet has as many as 17 billion cells. A number to make your head spin. Suffice it to say that if we were fast enough to enter, keeping the rate of one second per operation, one character into each cell, it would take us 545 years to fill the sheet.

Once we start Excel what we see is represented by Figure 1.1.

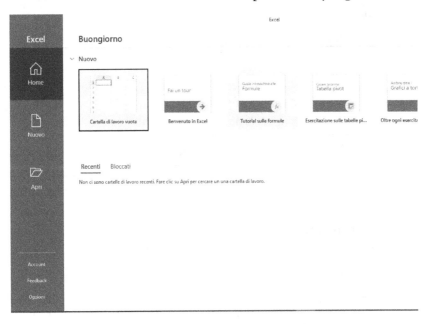

Figure 1.1 Excel Startup Panel

Once we are faced with the panel in Figure 1.1 we simply point and click our mouse on the New icon in the left column. What will appear on our screen will be Figure 1.2.

Figure 1.2 Screen shot of the New command.

Here we will simply click Empty Workbook and we will have our table displayed ready to receive the data we will need to enter.

In this panel you will also find the option to use or download Excel templates. What are these templates? Let's say they are an aid to getting started on a project. They are workbooks with their own predefined structure that can be, also depending on the project, simple or complex. They tend to be a valuable aid when we have to deal with projects that have a similar structure allowing us to save a lot of time.

Therefore, when we start the New command we know that our project, or our idea, can start from scratch or take advantage of a kind of predefined draft already that, of course, we can modify as we like.

14

Once we have created our worksheet and entered the data, we need to be able to save it in order either to reuse it or to continually update it. And this is where the Save command comes into the picture in all its importance.

Once we have completed our sheet, all we need to do is place the mouse in the upper left-hand corner and click on File in order to display the following screen. Alternatively, you can select the floppy disk icon located above the box that identifies which cell you are workingin.

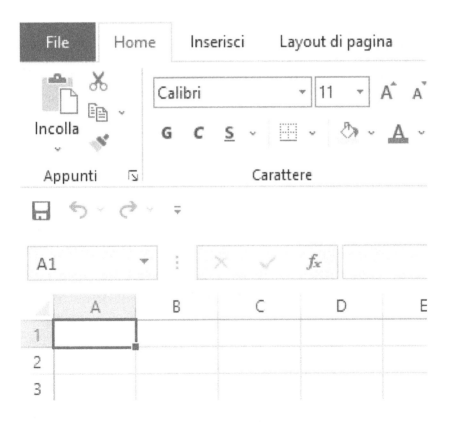

Figure 1.3 Save screen

Here we are faced with no less than three options.

Save: allows us to save our workbook directly by confirming the name we have chosen and the location where we have decided to save our workbook. If this is the first time we run it, the command will ask us where and under what name to save our file.

Save As: allows us to save our file with a name other than the preset name and to select the directory in which to place it. This is also the command used when we are unsure of the changes we have made to a sheet and prefer to save it under a different name thus creating a copy.

Save as Adobe PDF: allows you to save our project as a pdf file to allow it to be viewed by those who do not have Excel on their computer. Item you will have only if your computer has Adobe Acrobat Pro installed, Adobe's popular suite designed for creating and editing pdf files.

16

When we save our file, Excel provides us with a long list of formarti in which to store it on our computer. The default extension in which to save files in Excel is *.xlsx.

| Cartella di lavoro di Excel (*.xlsx) |
| Cartella di lavoro con attivazione macro di Excel (*.xlsm) |
| Cartella di lavoro binaria di Excel (*.xlsb) |
| Cartella di lavoro di Excel 97-2003 (*.xls) |
| CSV UTF-8 (delimitato da virgole) (*.csv) |
| Dati XML (*.xml) |
| Pagina Web in file unico (*.mht;*.mhtml) |
| Pagine Web (*.htm;*.html) |
| Modello di Excel (*.xltx) |
| Modello con attivazione macro di Excel (*.xltm) |
| Modello di Excel 97-2003 (*.xlt) |
| Testo (con valori delimitati da tabulazioni) (*.txt) |
| Testo Unicode (*.txt) |
| Foglio di calcolo XML 2003 (*.xml) |
| Cartella di lavoro di Microsoft Excel 5.0/95 (*.xls) |
| CSV (delimitato dal separatore di elenco) (*.csv) |
| Testo formattato (delimitato da spazio) (*.prn) |
| Testo (Macintosh) (*.txt) |
| Testo (MS-DOS) (*.txt) |
| CSV (Macintosh) (*.csv) |
| CSV (MS-DOS) (*.csv) |
| DIF (Formato interscambio dati) (*.dif) |
| SYLK (Connessione logica) (*.slk) |
| Componente aggiuntivo di Excel (*.xlam) |
| Componente aggiuntivo di Excel 97-2003 (*.xla) |
| PDF (*.pdf) |
| Documento XPS (*.xps) |
| Foglio di calcolo Open XML Strict (*.xlsx) |
| Formato ODS (*.ods) |

Figure 1.3.1 Save As

If you select Save as Adobe PDF you will get the following screen in Figure 1.4 that will allow you to save your file in pdf format with all the appropriate caveats.

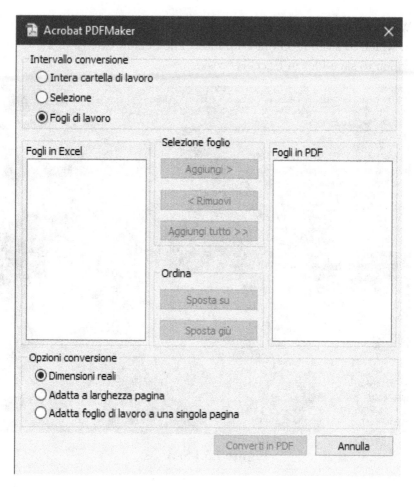

Figure 1.4 Save as Adobe PDF

Among the most interesting features is the one that allows you to fit the entire worksheet on a single page. Very convenient feature, but always remember that if your sheet is particularly rich in values, reading it on an A4 sheet may be difficult.

2. Customizing the work environment with toolbar management

Since the version of Excel 2007, Microsoft has introduced the ribbon bar-in the original language ribbon-that runs vertically, thus reducing the space available for the document window. In that bar are all the options for individual commands ranging from Home to What do you want to do? The Adobe command is found only after installing the Adobe Acrobat Pro software.

Figure 2.1 Excel Bar

If we felt that the size of the ribbon was somewhat intrusive, we would simply select with a click of the mouse the angular vertex icon that indicates the top and is located at the end of our ribbon to the right. If, on the other hand, we are in a hurry, we can use a trick that is employed by experts in the field and called a keyboard shortcut, that is, starting a command by selecting only a simple key combination. In this case, the combination we are interested in is Ctrl+F1.

If you select any of the sections of our ribbon, all you have to do is slide the mouse over any item for a box to appear explaining the function of the selected item. This is an extremely useful option should you find yourself in doubt as to exactly what a bar icon corresponds to.

The last bar to appear in the top band, and below the multifunction bar, is the formula bar. It cannot be minimized but can be enlarged by clicking on the button located on the far right in the shape of a downward arrowhead.

It is important to keep in mind that in such a bar only a formula is written and appears, for example (=A1+A2), while the result of that formula will be visible in the cell. On its left is visible a button with the mathematical symbol for the function $\int x$. A click on this button allows us to start a procedure for entering one of the very many functions available in Excel. At the beginning of our formula bar is placed a box called Name Box.

Here the name of the cell selected within the worksheet appears. The name, therefore, is defined by coordinates, e.g., A1 or C34, and it is also possible to write a name of convenience, such as the interval between several cells after selecting them.

The Name Box can also be used to move more easily to any cell on the worksheet.

At the bottom of our worksheet we find what is called the Status Bar as shown in Figure 2.2.

Figure 2.2 Status Bar

Under the name of the Sheet we find a message which, in the case of our figure, turns out to be accessibility is compliant. With this message, Excel is telling us that our worksheet is also accessible to people with different abilities.

The first icon on the right, in the shape of a grid, tells us the normal view of our worksheet, that is, the grid we see. The second one intervenes on the page layout by allowing us to add a header to our table, while the third one shows us the preview of the page break. This last view is very useful in the case of printing to assess what the last data will be printed at the end of the page and

20

allowing us to see if this does not harm the readability of our work.

At the end of our status bar we find a small scroll line that goes from - to +. Moving it to the left decreases the size of our worksheet, while moving to the plus increases its size.

3. Enter data correctly by formatting the cell according to the type of data entered

Each of the individual cells in a worksheet has a very large capacity of 32,767 characters i.e., to give you an idea of that magnitude, each cell could accommodate 9 to 10 pages of a book.

To enter data into a cell, one must select it with a click and then type the sequence of characters we are interested in, concluding that entry by pressing the Enter key.

The data entry must be extremely precise and written in the right format, otherwise Excel will signal us that we have made a mistake. In order to be sure of the format of the data we are going to enter, once we have selected the cell we simply enter our data and select a combination window, which we usually find on the Home tab of our Ribbon called General. In figure 3.1. you can see the effect of selecting this combination window along with its entries.

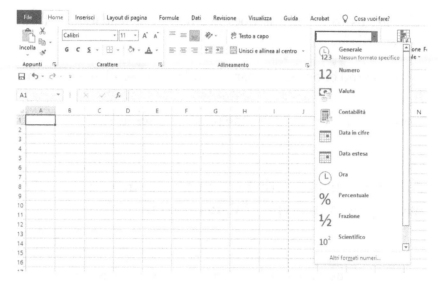

Figure 3.1 Data formatting

Making the click on the triangular vertex icon looking down opens the drop-down menu where we can choose the format of our data. If we are in doubt, it is best to leave the General format. Keep in mind that since this is a worksheet that processes data, the more precise you are in your input format the more accurate your work will be.

Trying to use the numbers 123456 as an example, you can see how their format changes depending on the option we choose as in Figure 3.2

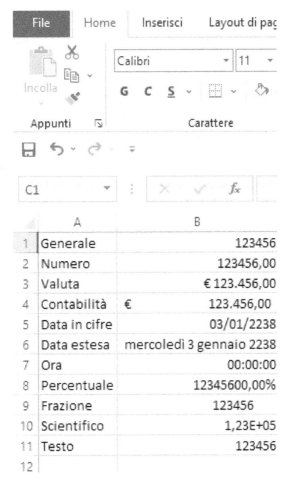

Figure 3.2 Data formatting example

Going into detail, we can say that formatting changes the display of the data in this way:

General: Applied to a number, displays it as it was written.

Number: Reduces any decimals by rounding them up. In case there were no decimals it adds two zeros after the decimal point.

Currency: Displays the financial currency symbol in front of the number entered; if the number was negative it puts the minus sign before the currency symbol.

Accounting: Similar to currency, moves the number one position to the left reflecting a format suitable for accounting entries.

Date in digits: Interprets the number as a date and expresses it in the compact form DD/MM/YYYYY.

Extended Date: This is like the date format only it indicates the day of the week and the name of the month in letters.

Time: Displays the number as an hour expressed in the hour, minute and second format.

Percentage: Displays the number in percentage format with two decimal places followed by the percentage symbol %.

Fraction: Displays the whole part of the number and presents the decimal part, if any, as a fraction.

Scientific: Represents the numerical value according to the convention called floating-point.

Text: Displays the data exactly as it was entered in the cell, but aligned to the left.

4. Select a cell and groups of cells, columns and rows

Selecting an individual cell is done simply by placing the mouse pointer over the individual cell with a click. In the upper left-hand corner, under the floppy icon (the floppy disk icon) you will be able to see the appearance of the cell's coordinate following its selection.

Alternatively, you can move by using the keyboard arrows found below the enter key and pressing Enter once you have reached the cell. Or again by moving thanks to the Tab key (the key the two arrows in the opposite direction that normally, on QWERTY keyboards is located to the left of theQ key) and once you have arrived at the cell press Enter.

But what if you want to select multiple cells? Nothing could be easier. We select a cell in the group we are interested in with the mouse pointer and, holding down the left mouse button, select all the contiguous cells we are interested in.

What if the cells I am interested in are not contiguous? No problem here either, we simply select the first cell with the mouse pointer and, while holding down the CTRL key, click on the individual cells that are the object of our attention.

What if the cell of my attention is an entire row or column? Again nothing could be easier. For the column we will simply position ourselves on the letter that identifies it with the mouse pointer and make a simple click, you will immediately notice that the entire column will be highlighted. Same for rows, we will simply position ourselves on the number that identifies the row and make a simple click to highlight it.

When working on cells that contain data, it may happen that we need to select the entire column very quickly. In the case, therefore, of a column that is decidedly rich in values or data, it is appropriate, or more convenient, to click on the first cell at the top; then, move the mouse pointer to the center of the bottom border, as a result of our action you will notice that our pointer will take the form of an arrow pointing in all four directions.

While holding down the Shift key (usually on QWERTY keyboards it is the key with the upward-pointing arrow next to the one with the angle brackets), double-clicking on the edge of the cell while the mouse pointer is in this particular shape will cause all the cells below in the column to be selected immediately, down to the last cell containing a value.

5. Perform copy/cut/paste operations

Regarding copy, cut and paste operations Excel is a Windows application, therefore, the key combinations we use for these commands in Windows also apply to Excel. That is, the following key combinations: Ctrl+C to copy; Ctrl+X to cut; and Ctrl+V to paste. You then simply position yourself on the cell you are interested in, apply the key combination you want, and position yourself on the target cell using the combination you need here as well.

Another method is to position yourself on the cell containing the data you are interested in, right-click and select one of two commands: Cut or Copy. Finally, position yourself on the cell where you want to return the data, press the right mouse button and select.

You may have noticed that our right-click action also produces a version of Paste that, to those unfamiliar with Excel, may seem like a novelty, namely the Paste Special command. Why would a program as powerful as Excel need this command that seems like an extension of the better known Paste? The need is there and it is concrete: not only numerical values or strings are stored in Excel cells, cells, as we have already seen, can also contain cross-references to other cells or even formulas and functions.

In the case of such a cell, using the paste command allows us to copy only the data expressed in the cell, while choosing Paste

Special allows us to copy the cross-reference to a cell or the function it may contain. Always keep this in mind when you want to move a cell that contains a formula or function that you have selected or processed.

6. Perform sorting operations.

Many times, caught up in the rush of entry, we do not ask ourselves the question of whether the data should be sorted or not, but having concluded the entry in our worksheet we may need our data to follow, either an alphabetical order, or a numerical order in order also to improve readability. But if the data is large in number, how can we solve this dilemma in a short time?

Simple, through the Sort and Filter command that we see in Figure 4.1

Figure 4.1 Sort and Filter

To sort our values we must select the cells that contain them and then choose one of the appropriate commands that appear and will be the subject of our choice:

Sort from Smallest to Largest: In numerical values it sorts from smallest to largest value. Texts, on the other hand, are sorted from A to Z.

Sort from Largest to Smallest: In numerical values it sorts from the largest value to the smallest value. Texts, on the other hand, are sorted from Z to A.

Custom sort: With this command we can customize the order of our data to our liking. By selecting it, the window in Figure 4.2 will appear.

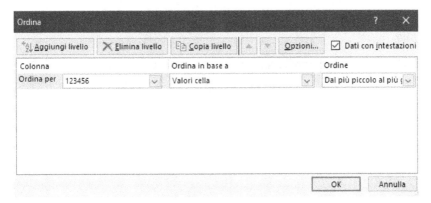

Figure 4.2 Custom sorting

Here we have three types of columns:

Sort by: if the general option is chosen then it means that the data are characters, while in 123456 we identify values in numbers. Depending on this choice the fields in the Order column change, of course.

Sort by: If we choose the Cell Values option we will be based on individual cell values; Cell Color means that our selection will be based on cell colors; Font Color will be a choice based on font color; and Conditional Formatting Icon based on particular icons that will be chosen depending on whether a particular value is part of a range type.

Order: Select the type of order we want. By size for numeric values, by color type, or alphabetical for characters.

7. Assign names to cells and groups of cells.

As you work on a certain amount of data, you will feel the need to accurately assign a name to a cell or even a group of cells. So far we know that a cell, or several cells, are identified by their coordinates (e.g. A1 or A1:A4).

As our project progresses it may happen that this mode of identification may, or may no longer be convenient for us, or we may no longer be able to identify the original data exactly. For this reason it would be good operational practice to assign a unique name to Excel cells thus also having the undoubted advantage of having indication of the type of data entered by means of the assigned name.

The procedure is very simple: to assign a name to a cell, or group of cells, one must select the cells that are of interest to us and go, within the ribbon, to the Formulas tab as depicted in Figure 4.3.

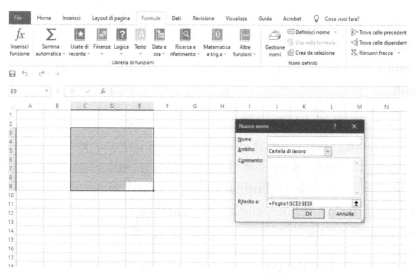

Figure 4.3 Naming cells.

In our example, the group of cells we are interested in is the one that extends from cell C3 down to cell E9. Once the Formulas tab is selected, we go with the pointer to Define Name and click.

Here a window opens that will allow you to name the group of cells-remember that it would be best to give a name that echoes the type of data we have entered-the scope where they will be saved, whether within the workbook or directly in the sheet. The space for comments is very useful because it allows you to memorize with great precision the meaning of your choice and the reference box where you are going to enter the range of cells that are the subject of the naming assignment.

It is important to know that this range will automatically appear to you in the window, but if by chance you want to add other cells to the range you can do so manually by changing the relevant coordinates.

A useful and valuable concept that you should always keep in mind is that the name you are going to choose must begin with a letter, and you will not be able to use spaces or report cell coordinates. Of course, you will be able to use letters, numbers and dots for the remaining characters in the name.

8. Change the formatting of individual cells or groups of cells.

If after entering data into our worksheet we realize that perhaps it was better if some cells were formatted differently, we can run for cover without the slightest effort and without fear of having to start all over again.

We will simply select the cells to which we want to change the formatting, hover with the cursor over the toolbar, move to Number, and by clicking on the triangular icon with the vertex turning down next to General, select the Other Formats item. Here the window in Figure 4.4 will appear.

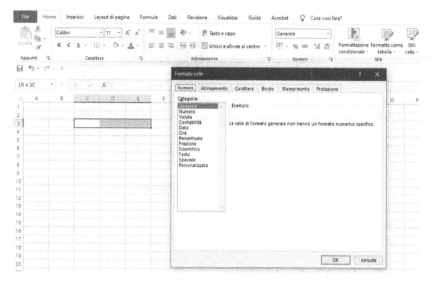

Figure 4.4 Edit cell formatting

Here you will find the following tabs:

Number: will allow you to change the format of the values you enter as we have already explained in section 3.

Alignment: you will be able to choose the best alignment to represent your data within the selected cells, both for horizontal and vertical, and decide the indentation space. Not only that, you will also be able to decide the degree of text orientation and text control.

Font: You can decide to change everything about the font, from the font type to its size. Choose the style, color, underline type and effects.

Border: in this tab you can choose how to display the cell borders, from all to none; choose the color of the borders themselves or even customize them.

Fill: this is the "artistic" tab, here you can choose the fill colors for the cells you select and also color them with the various drawing styles.

Protection: is the most delicate tab, here you can choose whether the selected cells can be locked, that is, not editable. Remember that this choice will only take effect if the worksheet has been protected.

In case you need worksheet protection, simply locate yourself in the Review tab of our ribbon and, inside the box. Protect you will find two commands: protect sheet and protect workbook. With the first command we will perform the protection of our worksheet, a special window will appear where we will be asked to enter the password for the protection (of our choice and possibly alphanumeric) and a series of options to be selected to indicate which parts of our sheet will be protected.

At this point our sheet is protected thus allowing us to enter or edit data only in the cells for which the checkbox has been unchecked. Folder protection will be more straightforward, having to protect the entire workbook you will only be required to enter a password, again of your choice.

Choice that must be judicious and well thought out as far as a password is concerned. The password could be described as a kind of cornerstone of computer security systems. Today we use them without problem because we are in contact with them every day, but their creation requires observance of certain rules that we might call common sense.

- Use, as a password, a string that is longer than six characters. Remember that Excel accepts passwords that can be up to 255 characters long;

- Never use meaningful phrases or names, especially names or places;

- Never use birth dates or dates of events that may be known to others;

- Passwords should always be alphanumeric, i.e., have both numbers and characters within them and perhaps special characters such as dollar or hash marks;

- Always use upper and lower case letters.

9. Set up simple arithmetic formulas

The real power of Excel lies not only in the easy entry of data and its orderly and graphical representation, but its real strength, that is, the real reason we use it, is in its computational power, which turns out to be easy and intuitive.

Excel is like a real scientific calculator capable of giving you, and subsequently storing in cells, the result of even complex calculations. In our worksheet we can create simple arithmetic formulas that allow us to do addition (+), subtraction (-), multiplication (*) and division (/). Let's try a simple example:

We select any cell on our worksheet and, curious about the result of addition between 3 and 8 we type the equal sign (=) followed by 3+8. At this point we need only press the Enter key to see the result inside our cell. Of course, the process is the same for all other arithmetic operators.

Let us try two operators: select any cell within our worksheet and type the following formula =3+8*2. The result will be 19, this is because Excel first multiplies 8 with 2 and then adds 3. What if I want to first add the 3 and the 8 and multiply by 2? Then we would simply have to introduce an important element of Excel formulas, the use of parantheses. In this case we would simply type = (3+8) *2 and get 22.

What if my data were in different cells? Here again the whole thing is now quite intuitive for us. Choose a cell in which you want to store the total and then simply, instead of typing values, use the cell coordinates. For example, let us assume that in cell A1 is stored (or allocated as it is used in more technical terms) the value 3, in A2 we have the value 7, and in cell A3 we have 10. We will place ourselves in cell A4 for convenience, but you can choose any cell you want, and we will type =A1+A2+A3 and get 20.

What if there are a lot of values? One of the virtues of the power of Excel is also automation. If we find ourselves needing to sum several values in a column, we can use the Auto Sum (Σ) command.

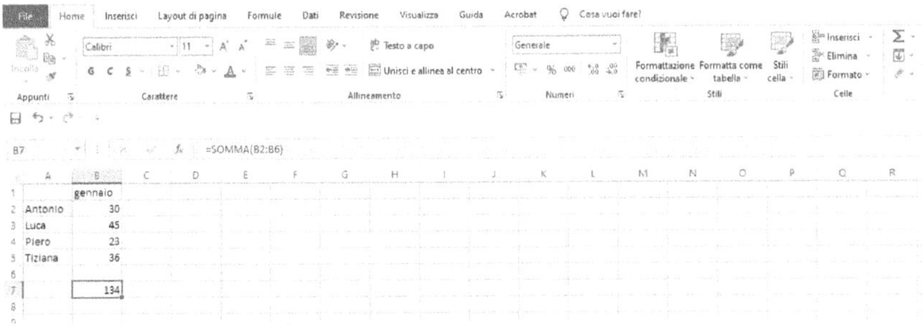

Figure 4.5 Automatic Sum

You will find this command at the end of the ribbon positioned at the top of the toolbar on the Home tab.

The operation is very simple and intuitive: select the cell that is to accommodate within it the sum of the values, click automatic sum, press Enter, and you will immediately have the total. Of course automatic sum is a command that takes a simple formula that we have already used.

It will not have escaped the notice of the more intuitive that, instead of using automatic sum, we could have created a formulated sum using cell coordinates, but here, to narrow the formula itself, we can select the range by changing the formula to the following =SUM(B2:B6). The colon indicates a continuous interval, that is, from cell B2 to cell B6, and SUM indicates a variable that we will soon get to know.

All this is to make you understand that a program like Excel can do the same thing in different ways; it is up to us, depending on our project and what we want to accomplish, to use the way we think is most suitable and, why not, fastest.

10. Uses of the fill handle

As we mentioned earlier, the advantage of using powerful software such as Excel lies in speeding up processes that we find tedious or unnecessarily time-consuming. Let us try, for the purpose of bringing an example to life, to think of having to enter the same numerical value a number of times or, even, having to manually enter a scale of numerical values.

As long as there are only a few we can think of manually entering them one at a time, but what if these values were an extremely large number? We have no choice but to use a technique made available by Excel: the fill handle.

The fill handle is a cell-filling technique that allows us to place the same value in an indefinite number of cells or to create a numerical scale in succession. Let's say we need to repurpose a number, in this case let's assume the number 1 six times. How can we do this without having to write down the number for all these times?

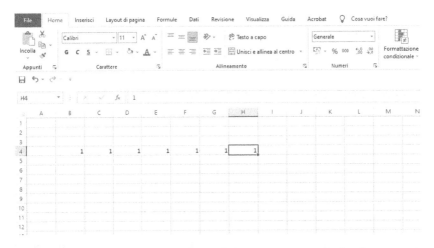

Figure 4.6 Reproduction of the same numerical value

We select our cell and type the number 1, then place our cursor in the right corner of the cell until the pointer turns into a cross. At this point, while holding down the left mouse button, scroll in any direction you want and then release, you will have obtained a sequence of numbers 1 without having to type it in as well depicted in Figure 4.6

But what if we find ourselves in the situation of needing to enter a number sequence? No problem, you will just select the cell where you will enter the starting value, say 0, move the pointer to the bottom corner of the cell until it takes the shape of a cross, press the CTRL button and the left mouse button moving along the line we want.

If we move to the right of the value the sequence will be increasing, if we move to the left it will be decreasing. Same thing if we moved up (decreasing) or down (increasing) as depicted in Figure 4.7.

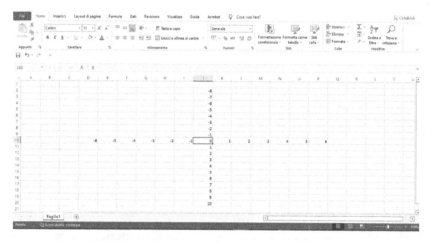

Figure 4.7 Increasing or decreasing series

Excel Intermediate Level

Creating tables

Formatting tables.

Creating and formatting an Excel table is a very important step. Entering data as if it were a simple list without taking care of its form or appearance risks making reading the table cumbersome and uncomfortable. Therefore, it is important to know how to format with the right combination of styles the data in our project also to allow, at a glance, to grasp the meaning of the relationships that emerged from our data.

After we have entered the data we are interested in, we select a cell within it, then we locate ourselves on the Home tab of our ribbon and click on Format as Table. What you will see is depicted by Figure 5.1.

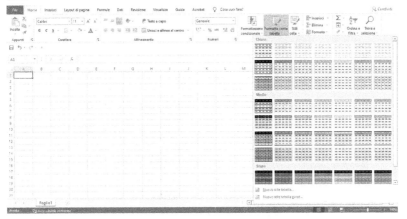

Figure 5.1 Table Formatting

The window that opens will show various predefined styles ranging from light through medium to dark. The styles have various colors alternating within them by varying the shade. The choice of style, as we mentioned earlier, must be chosen wisely. The style should allow for emphasis on the type of data we are interested in having the most visibility and allow for smooth reading. A well-formatted table must be readable at a glance. Well-defined formatting is the basis of that data analysis that we will get to see later; therefore, it is an essential basic step.

In case none of the listed styles work for us, we can click on the New Table Style item to be able to see what is displayed in Figure 5.2.

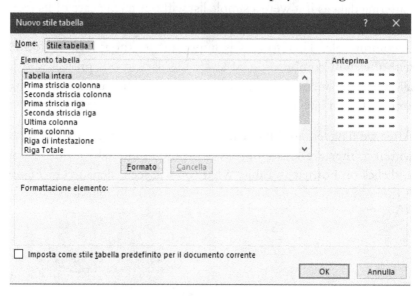

Figure 5.2 New table style

When the window opens we find the name box, in which to enter the name to the new style we are creating. Again, it would be appropriate if the name chosen could refer to the type of style we plan to create. Then, once we are positioned in the individual entries in the Table Element list, we place the pointer on Format and click.

This action will open three tabs that we have previously learned about: font, border and fill. We select the tones and features that we like best, but most importantly that may be most functional for our project, and after clicking ok we will return to our table to modify other elements that we consider important.

Obviously, the more items we keep in mind, the more our style will be completed. Be careful, however, not to overdo it because this could lead to a decrease in the readability of our table generating confusion when reading.

If we are satisfied with our new style, we can put a check mark - by clicking on the white square - on the item Set as default table style for the current document so that our style is immediately operational and visible.

The last item is New Pivot table style whose style selection is identical to the previous item. As for what the Pivot table may be, suffice it for now to know that this will be the subject of clarification and further discussion in a future section.

Using the total row to summarize data.

As we enter our data into the worksheet we may need to have a summary of the data, perhaps a partial sum so that we can understand the trend of our figures and data. To get this quickly we can take advantage of an option in Excel called a total row.

To perform it we need to select a cell, this action will activate a tab in the toolbar called table tools as in figure 5.3.

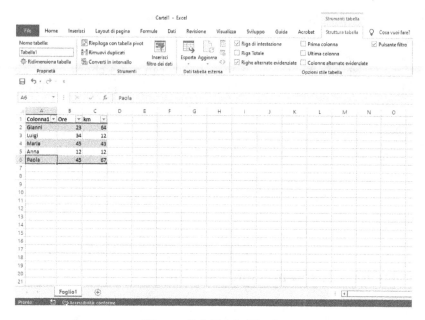

Figure 5.3 Table Tools

Now simply place the mouse pointer over Total Row and click, obtaining the screen in Figure 5.4.

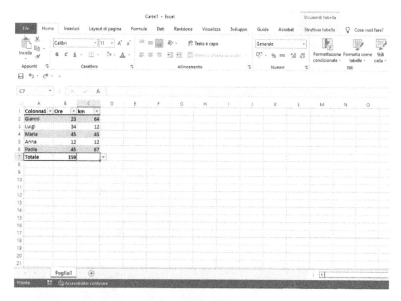

Figure 5.4 Total row

A row will appear at the end of the table where, at the bottom of each column, a box will be created flanked by a triangle with the vertex at the bottom indicating a drop-down menu.

This is because Total Row not only allows us to have the sum of our data but also a number of functions that we can see in Figure 5.5.

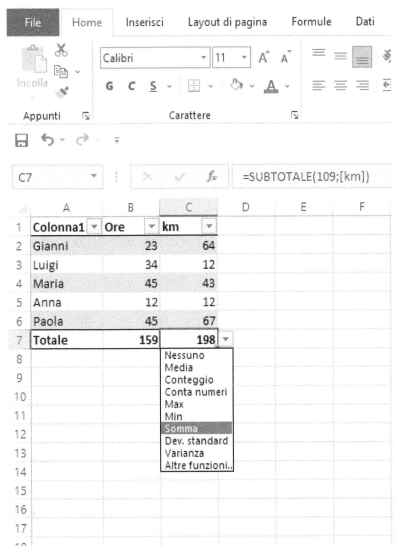

Figure 5.5 Total Row Options

Delete duplicate values from a table

Eliminating duplicate values can be very useful because it allows on the one hand the lightening of the weight of our file and a better synthesis of our table. Moreover, the elimination of these values, as we will get to see later when we talk about data analysis, allows Excel to process our data more smoothly and quickly.

However, it should not be forgotten that this is an operation that can also result in the loss of data that could be useful to us instead, so it should be used well and with some caution.

The first operation to do, having a table with a certain amount of values, is to identify them precisely, perhaps color them so that this data jumps out at us immediately, but how to do it? Thanks to conditional formatting.

Let us go to the toolbar and in particular to the Home tab where we are going to select the conditional formatting command, obtaining what can be seen from Figure 5.6.

Figure 5.6 Conditional formatting

Now we click on duplicate values to get the window in Figure

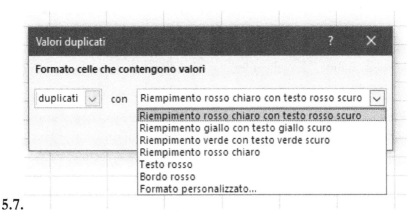

Riempimento rosso chiaro con testo rosso scuro
Riempimento giallo con testo giallo scuro
Riempimento verde con testo verde scuro
Riempimento rosso chiaro
Testo rosso
Bordo rosso
Formato personalizzato...

5.7.

Figure 5.7 Coloring options for duplicate values.

Having reached this point, all we have to do is choose the type of highlighting of this duplicate data and then press the Enter key or, with the left mouse button, click Ok.

At this point Excel will highlight within our table the duplicate values. Highlighting them before removing them is important because Excel may highlight two values, for example, equal to 0 but which in reading the data identify two totally different situations.

Once we have ascertained, thanks to the highlighting provided by conditional formatting, what the duplicate values are, we can begin to remove them. Again use the utmost caution and care, it is advisable to back up the data before coming to the removal operation this because with this option the data will be removed permanently.

Once the duplicate data has been selected, there will be nothing left for us to do but delete it after carefully reviewing it.

Sort data by the contents of one or more columns

Sorting data well is a key feature with regard to readability and analysis of projects in Excel. A well-ordered and formatted project can really make a difference. If on the one hand you have failed to sort them, perhaps to speed up entry or because the project has been edited by several hands, Excel gives us the opportunity to do so and automatically without taking too long in unnecessary steps.

Let us select the column, or columns, that we are interested in sorting. After that, let us position ourselves in the ribbon on the Data tab. Now all we will have to do is select the type of sorting we need as pictured in Figure 6.1.

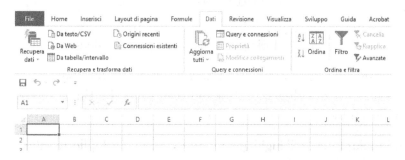

Figure 6.1 Sorting Data

If we select the AZ icon with the arrow pointing down, this will allow us to distribute our jobs in alphabetical order (A to Z) or, if they are numerical values, in ascending order from smallest to largest. If, on the other hand, our choice falls on the ZA icon with the arrow always pointing down, we will have our data sorted, again alphabetically, from Z to A, while the numerical ones will be in descending order, that is, from largest to smallest.

The last icon, the square with the letters ZA and AZ above the name. Sort, allows us to have the same effects as the main commands but in a more complete and precise way. By clicking on it we get what is represented by Figure 6.2.

48

Figure 6.2 Data Sort window

The Sort Data window gives us a wider range of options to choose from. We can sort our data by Column or by the values in our cell. If we perform a click on the drop-down menu (the corner icon with the vertex at the bottom at the end of the box) we will have more options, and more precisely: cell color if we want to sort according to how we have colored our cells; font color according to the font coloring used in our cells or conditional formatting icon depending on the condition applied to the cells.

Finally, thanks to the last box, we can choose whether to sort our values from smallest to largest, largest to smallest or by custom list. This last item allows us to create our own preferred order to apply to our values in case we do not think the other options are appropriate.

Filter data by one or more criteria.

When using a table in our worksheet to capture data, it may happen that as time passes, and as new values are entered, new rows may be added, thus increasing the size of the table. The large number of rows greatly complicates the identification of values by simple sorting. It is at this point that the feature called Filter becomes valuable and important, accessible with the Filter command within the Data tab of the Ribbon as can be seen in Figure 7.1.

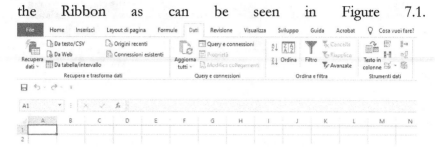

Figure 7.1 Filter

After selecting our table, all we have to do is click on the Filter command so that, at the label of each column, a combo box (the box with a triangle positioned with the vertex at the bottom) is displayed, the contents of which become visible as soon as we click on the same triangle as we can view in Figure 7.2 and Figure 7.3

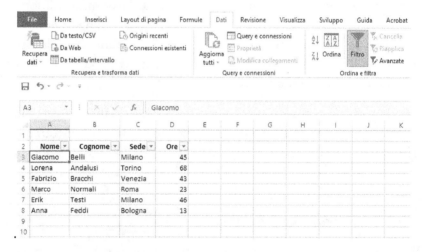

Figure 7.2 Filter Activation

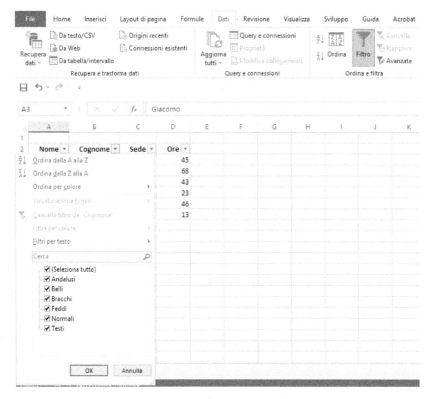

Figure 7.3 Filter Options

Each drop-down list of the combined boxes presents various options, some of which we got to see when we talked about sorting data in the previous section.

Further down, on the other hand, we find the Filter by Text command, which has, in turn, as many as seven entries with which particular logical conditions can be defined, ranging from Equal to

Custom Filter, which are visible in Figure 7.4.

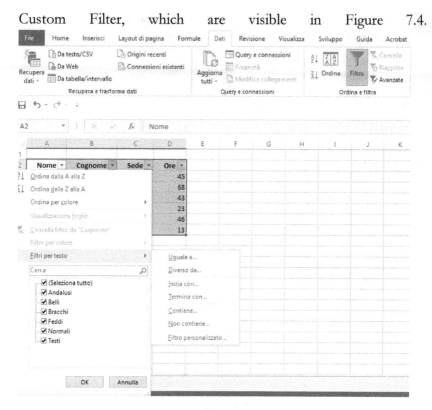

Figure 7.5 Filter by Text

In the final part of the window, we find several check boxes, more specifically one for each data item in the column we selected. Unchecking a value means making it no longer visible in the Column, that is, filtering it.

Mind you, this process does not delete the value row, but simply hides it from view. To return to making it visible we will simply select the value again or click Select All.

In the toolbar, at the bottom left, there will appear, based on the values you have selected, the number of records, or values, that will correspond to what you have chosen to filter.

If, on the other hand, we wanted to select a column containing only numeric values, our menu would be Filter by Numbers as in Figure

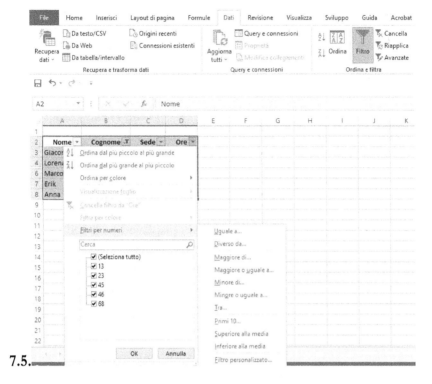

Figure 7.5 Filter by numbers

Filter by Numbers adds three subcommands to the previous filter namely First 10..., Above Average, and Below Average.

The subcommand First 10... allows to activate a window called Automatic First 10 Filter where it is possible to select either the highest first ten values or the lowest first ten values of the entire column under consideration.

By acting on the right-hand box we have the possibility of selecting, or considering, the highest or the lowest values not according to their absolute value, but with reference to a percentage of the total available values as in Figure 7.6.

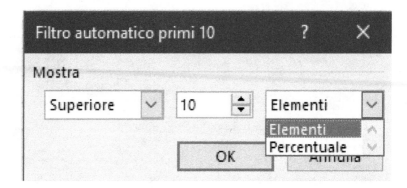

Figure 7.6 Automatic filter first 10

It should be pointed out that the rows displayed with the First 10... command will not appear based on the value we selected, but it will be possible to sort them by selecting them and choosing the Sort command found within the Data tab of our Ribbon.

The Custom Filter subcommand allows us to bring to life particular filters that are based on logical expressions that are also quite complex. Once activated, the Customize Automatic Filter window opens as you can see from Figure 7.7.

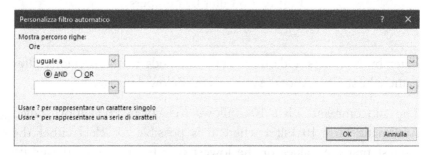

Figure 7.7 Custom Filter

The Customize Automatic Filter window allows you to create one or two selection criteria. If we wanted to create two, for example, they can be combined with the logical AND operator or, conversely, use the logical OR operator so that the condition of only one value is met.

Recall that the logical AND operator is a conjunction operator between two logical propositions. The logical OR operator, on the other hand, is a disjunction or separation operator between two logical propositions.

You can thus create a custom filter even on a field that contains text values by typing into the text entry box (the one on the right in our example) a string to search within the selected field.

There is also one last option for filtering data, a more complex one called Advanced.

To activate it we need to select the Data tab of our ribbon and click on the Advanced command. That command allows us to define a selection criterion, which is clearly more complex and based on multiple comparison criteria referring to multiple columns. You can see such a window in figure 7.8.

Figure 7.8 Advanced Filter

The Advanced Filter requires extra attention. The selection criterion must be created preliminarily in any location on the sheet, preferably outside the table we are considering.

At a minimum, a criterion consists of a column name and a value, which must be on two overlapping cells. Therefore, taking two cells into consideration, the first should contain the name of the column we are interested in, while the second may contain a string of characters, a numerical value or a date. The coordinates of the two cells should be entered in the Criteria Range box.

In the box that will eventually contain a string, you can also use so-called wildcard characters such as * and ? For example, if we wanted to do a search in the Last Name column we would type this name in the first cell and, in the second, we would type our option which could be this: *mm*. That is, we are asking to consider all surnames of any length and name as long as they contain the double m.

The window contains two options, one called Filter the list in place (this is the default and causes rows that do not match our criteria to be hidden) and the other is Copy to another location. Choosing it makes available a third Copy in text box in which you can type in the extremes that identify a new range in which to get copies of the filtered cells.

The last box, the one called Unique Record Copy, allows us to determine whether we wish to have a copy of all records that meet our filtering criteria or whether duplicates are allowed.

Graphs

A graph is nothing more than a drawing of a geometric type representing one or more relationships between one or more series of values. Therefore, the fundamental element of a graph cannot but be the series of data to be represented thus bringing its purpose to be that of showing differences between the data of one series and those of another.

The data that will be of interest to our graph are represented, using different techniques, which we will go on to see, on a geometric plane called the Plot Area, bounded by two axes, one vertical called the y-axis and one horizontal, the x-axis.

Histograms

Histograms, or otherwise known as column graphs, are among the most popular and easiest graphs to understand and construct. Data are represented as vertical columns whose height is defined by the value of each data item considered. To create a histogram, we will simply locate ourselves on the Insert tab of the Ribbon and then locate ourselves on Graphs. Here we will simply select the column icon as depicted in figure 8.1.

Figure 8.1 Graphs

The graph will be filled in automatically and will be displayed next to our Table as shown in Figure 8.2.

Figure 8.2 Histograms

Positioning within the chart and clicking will activate two new tabs in the ribbon: chart structure and format depicted by the illustrations in Figure 8.3 and Figure 8.4.

Figure 8.3 Graphic structure

Figure 8.4 Format

In the two new tabs that are created you can customize the chart has your liking, from the colors to the style of the columns, with the possibility of integrating the legend and titles of the chart or inverting the columns. You can also have the chart in a 3D version.

Pie charts

The pie chart is employed as a depiction of the relative proportions of the data in a series, that is, their percentage incidence in relation to the sum of all values in the series.

It should be dutifully mentioned that such a representation is useful and effective only if the number of values that make up the series is not large, say no more than five or six slices (or slices of pie as it is more commonly said), otherwise, if the values to be represented were very high, the result would be difficult to read.

We can see a clear example of this in figure 8.5.

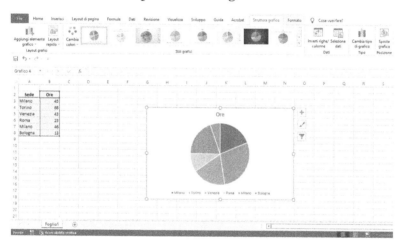

Figure 8.5 Diagramma a Torta

Stacked bar graphs

Stacked bar graphs are actually nothing more than histograms with the columns arranged horizontally. Such a graph is often preferred to the histogram when the labels describing the data are particularly long and thus would struggle to be represented with any readability at the base of the histogram columns.

An example of a bar graph is presented in Figure 8.6.

Figure 8.6 Stacked bar graphs

Line Charts

Line graphs depict one or more sets of data as lines joining points that identify values in the plane of the graph. They are predominantly used to represent long-lived phenomena over time and to indicate trends.

A line graph is that in Figure 8.7

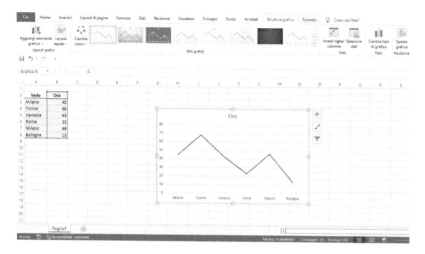

Figure 8.7 line graph

Area Graphs

The area chart is simply a line graph with the part below the line filled in a different color for each series. It is extremely useful for identifying data trends over time.

Figure 8.8 is an example.

Figure 8.8 Area Graphs

Radar Charts

The radar chart gets this name from the fact that many times, graphically, they take on the appearance of a radar antenna because they use a separate axis for each category, and these axes diversify starting from the center of the chart. Each value, therefore, is plotted on the corresponding axis. They are important because they make it possible to represent multiple data sets that are correlated with each other.

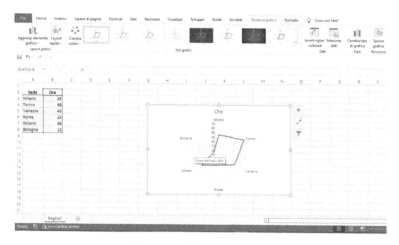

Figure 8.9 Radar Charts

Sparkline charts

An important feature of Excel is that it allows the creation of so-called sparkline charts, which are miniature charts based on a single set of data and contained entirely in a single cell.

To create a sparkline graph, one must go to the Insert tab of the ribbon and, in the Sparkline Graphs section, choose one of the three graph types present: Lines, Histogram, and Positive/Negative.

At this point a window called Create sparkline graphs will appear where you will have to indicate the range of data to be represented, once you have identified the position in which to create the sparkline graph, which must be in the active worksheet, you press the OK button with the left mouse button.

At this point the sparkline graph we requested can be displayed. An example can be seen in Figure 8.10.

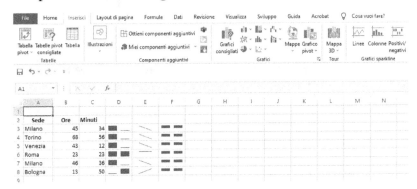

Figure 8.10 Sparkline charts

2D and 3D graphs

All the graphs we have examined have one representative feature: they are 2D graphs.

Excel, however, being a powerful management program allows you to make 3D charts as well. All charts, especially histograms and pie charts, can also be depicted in three-dimensional versions. You only need to select the 3D version within the submenus of the various types of graphs. Figure 8.11and 8.12 show you the selection and a graph in 3D version.

Figure 8.11 3D Graph Selection

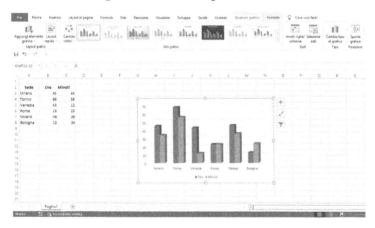

Figure 8.12 3D Graph

Formulas

Previously, we mentioned formulas that can be entered into cells obtaining an immediate result. It should be pointed out that such a result can be obtained by combining the cell number with a given value.

If we had, for example, the need to have in a given cell the value of another cell multiplied by 10 we would simply position ourselves on the cell that is to contain the result, let us say it is cell B3 and write inside it the following formula: = A1*10 where A1 is the cell in which we typed the value we are interested in multiplying.

The advantage of using this formula is that it allows us, by changing only one value, to always have a new and updated result.

In the formulas we can, of course, use all the arithmetic operators of our knowledge such as addition, subtraction, multiplication, division and power elevation. Not only that, but we can also write formulas that do not deal with numeric data but also with strings that may be in various cells.

The arithmetic operators used in Excel are as follows:

Sum +;

Subtraction -;

Multiplication *;

Division /;

Power elevation ^.

In case we are faced with two strings, for example, we can use the & operator to join them. Assume we have in cell A1 the name Mario and in cell B1 the name Bianchi. If we are interested in having in a cell where the first name and the last name will be stored together, all we need to do is to position ourselves in cell C! and type the following formula = A1 & " " & B1.

You may have noticed that there is a space in the formula, that is to remind Excel to put a space between the first and last name, otherwise they would be written without separation but contiguous

Functions

We have talked about formulas, but what are functions? And why is it important to know them?

Functions are predefined formulas that are identified by Excel by a keyword followed by round brackets. Inside those brackets are the arguments, sometimes also called function parameters, that is, the data on which the function is called to act.

The first, very simple function we are going to learn about is the SUM() function, which we already had a chance to see when we talked about the automatic sum.

SUM()

The SUM() function is perhaps by far the most widely used function in Excel. It returns, in the cell where it is entered, the result of summing all the data contained in the range of cells indicated inside the parentheses as the function argument.

For example, the following function =SUM(A1:C10) calculates the sum of the values contained in cells ranging from A1 to C10. Beware, if by chance in any cells in the range considered there were not numbers but strings, these would be ignored. Always remember that strings are alphabetical series.

But what if we want to calculate the sum of all the values contained in column B? Simple and straightforward, you will simply type =SUM(B:B). Easy and intuitive will also be the procedure in case we want to sum all the elements of a row, let's say we are interested in row 5, we will just type =SUM(5:5).

As you can see, knowing how to use intervals is extremely convenient, as well as being a wild card in long and complex situations, to the extent that our project will increasingly increase the number of data elements to be considered.

In Excel, when it comes to functions, you will always have to type "=" and begin typing the first letter to get the program's suggestions by immediately presenting you with a list of functions that reflect the parameters you are typing.

SUMIF()

SUMIF() is a function that is part of the mathematics and trigonometry category group and allows us to obtain in a cell, where this function is inserted, the sum of only the numeric values present in a given range of cells, which could also have empty cells or cells with alphabetic strings.

The syntax (i.e., the form in which this function is written) provides three arguments, two of which are absolutely mandatory:

SUMIF(range; criterion; [int_sum])

By range of course we refer to the entire range of cells that is to be considered, while criterion determines how the cells specified in the range are to be selected. The last argument specifies a range to sum other than interval; if we decide to omit it (as mentioned it is optional), all the values of the cells indicated in interval will be summed.

Let's take a brief example; let's assume that given a number of students who need tutoring in certain subjects, we want to calculate the total number of hours that have been taken to make up any deficiencies in mathematics. Figure 9.1 clarifies the mechanism:

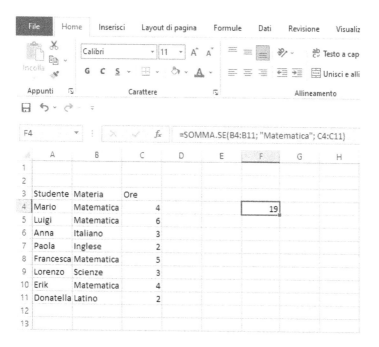

Figure 9.1 SUMIF()

As you can see from the view, it is extremely important to be precise with the cell ranges and with the argument, which must be written between superscripts and in the same way as it is written at the top of the column.

SUMIFS ()

Unlike SUMIF(), the function SUMIFS() allows us to sum values that meet more than one criteria, if you like it is somewhat the plural of the previous function.

The syntax is as follows:

SUMIFS(int_sum; interval_criteria1; criteria1; [interval_criteria2; criteria2]; ...)

Here the interval to be the subject of the sum is the first argument of the function, followed by the criterion interval and the criterion itself.

In Figure 9.2 you can see an example of such a function.

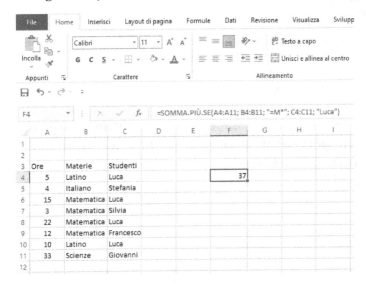

Figure 9.2 SUMIFS()

This time we were keen to know how many hours of repetition in mathematics the student Luca had. As can be seen from the example, as a criterion for Mathematics we typed M followed by *, obviously this was done to speed up the writing knowing that the only subject present that began with M was indeed Mathematics.

If, however, Music had also been there, the criterion would have led the function to add up those hours as well. Remember, therefore, to always be extremely precise in writing the criterion.

COUNTIF ()

The COUNTIF () function is actually a statistical function and allows us to count the number of values that match a given criterion. This is the syntax:

COUNTIF (range; criterion)

Where range is the set of cells we want to consider for the function and criterion indicates which of those cells will be counted.

Figure 9.3 shows us this function.

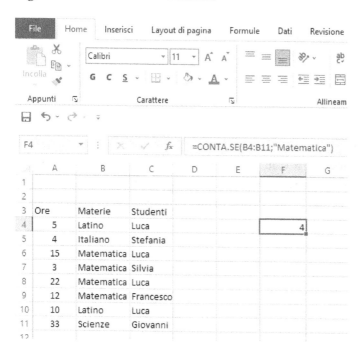

Figure 9.3 COUNTIF

As can be seen from the formula, we asked the function to count the numbers of cells in column B containing the subject Math.

AVERAGE ()

The AVERAGE() function, as the name makes clear, allows us to know the average value from a list of values in a given column. This is the syntax:

AVERAGE(num1; [num2]; ...)

Where num1 indicates either a number or the reference cell.

For example, if we wanted to calculate the average of the first twenty numbers in column A, this would be the correct function: = AVERAGE(A1:A20).

LOOKUP ()

LOOKUP () is a search function, based on a given criterion it tells me who a given value matches.

Its syntax is this:

LOOKUP (value, vector, [result])

Where value is the value we are looking for within vector and can be either a number or a value, vector can contain a row or a column, result on the other hand is a range of row or column in which the data corresponding to value we are looking for is found. Figure 9.4 is an example of this.

Figure 9.4 LOOKUP ()

In this case, we asked our function to look for the student who had done only three hours of repetition.

VLOOKUP()

The VLOOKUP () function allows us, unlike the previous one, to search within multiple rows or columns. This is its syntax:

VLOOKUP (value; matrix_table; index; [range])

Where value is the value to be searched within our data, matrix_table is the range of cells in which the value will be searched (this range can also correspond to an entire table).

Index is the column number that contains within it the value to be returned (always remember that we start from the leftmost column which is column A) and range, which is optional, indicates the logical value that indicates whether we want to discover an exact or approximate match.

SEARCH ()

The SEARCH () function is constructed very simply, that is, it requires knowing two parameters: what we are searching for and where we are searching for it. Its syntax is as follows:

SEARCH (text;string;[start])

Text is the text, number or sequence that is the subject of our search, string indicates the range in which our search will be performed, and start optionally allows us to enter a character that must be present in our result.

An example of a function is the following: = SEARCH ("i"; A2;8). This function tells us the position number of the letter i contained in the string in cell A2 beginning with the eighth character.

RIGHT()

The RIGHT() function is used to receive a given number the characters, from a string, starting from the end.

Its notation is as follows:

RIGHT(text;[num_caratt])

In text will be entered the number of the cell containing the string of our interest, while in num_caratt we will enter the number of characters we want to extract.

Let's say that cell A2 contains the string Silvia, if we write the following function = RIGHT (A2;1) the resulting result will bring back the character a, that is, the last letter of the string Silvia.

Keep in mind that if you decide to omit the number of characters, Excel will automatically return the last character of the string.

LEFT()

In a totally complementary way, the LEFT() function allows you to extract the leftmost characters of a certain cell.

Its notation will thus turn out to be as follows:

LEFT(text;[num_caratt])

By text we mean the coordinate of the cell containing the string of our interest, and by num_caratt the number of characters we want to extract.

Keeping with the example given with the RIGHT function of a cell A2 containing the string Silvia, in this case typing the following function. = LEFT (A2;1) the result we will get will be the letter s.

DATE()

The DATE() function is among the richest functions in Excel, it goes up to about twenty sub-functions. Let us now see what it consists of and what the most important ones are.

First, we must remember that the moment, in a cell we write the string 27/03/2022 this is immediately recognized by Excel as a date, so much so that the program immediately changes the format of the cell from General to Date.

The function DATE () returns to us the sequential number representing a unique date thus allowing us to perform operations on dates.

The syntax of the function is:

DATE (year;month;day)

The identification and meaning of the arguments is itself intuitive.

If we want to know today's date accurately, we need only type the =TODAY() function into a cell and Excel will display the date of the day.

Important is the DATEVALUE() function, which allows us to convert a date stored in a cell as a serial number, thus enabling us to perform certain operations, including filtering data.

To obtain the serial value of a date simply use the following syntax:

DATEVALUE(date)

If we typed in any cell the function = DATEVALUE ("27/03/2022") we would get as a result its serial number, which is 44647.

IF()

The IF() function is one of the most famous functions in Excel along with SUM(). Here we are in the field of conditional and logical and it allows to obtain are two types of results: true or false.

In fact, this function allows you to perform a logical comparison between a value and a result.

Its syntax therefore will be as follows:

IF(test; if_true;if_false).

Where test represents a comparison operation, if_true will be the value that will be returned if the comparison has generated a logical true value, if_false on the other hand if the value is false.

Assume we have a box such as A3 in which there is the value 20 and enter, in an empty box, the following function: = IF((A8>10; "True"). The result of that function will be the appearance of the word True in our cell.

In its simplicity, the IF() function is extraordinarily important in Excel because it allows the construction of even much more complex formulas beginning with nested formulas.

ISERROR()

This function allows us to know whether a value, or an expression, supplied may return an error. Therefore, its syntax will be as follows:

ISERROR(value)

Where value identified the cell coordinate in which the value we want to parse or a string is enclosed.

The value return will be true if there is an error, while it will verge to false if there is no error of any kind in our cell.

INDEX()

The INDEX() function allows us to achieve a value from a range or an entire table, based on position.

This is its syntax:

INDEX (array; row; [col])

Array means a range of cells; row is the position of the row in our reference and col is the position of the column.

Therefore, if we wrote the following function = INDEX (A1:C11;5;3) we would get the value contained in cell C5 that is the one located at the fifth row and third column.

MATCH ()

The MATCH () function allows us to search for a given element within a range thus returning the relative position of that element. Its syntax is as follows:

MATCH (value; array; [corrisp])

With value we search for the matching datum within our array. If our matrix were a set of addresses and we would like to find the ZIP code, the person's last name would be the search value, while the ZIP code of his address would be the desired value. It should be specified that value can be a number, a cell, text or a logical value.

Matrix is nothing but the range of cells within which our search will be carried out; corrisp, which is optional, indicates how Excel should compare the value argument with those contained in the matrix.

Let us clarify the function with an example: assume that the range A1:A3 includes values 8, 12 and 40, the formula = MATCH (12;A1:A3;0) will return the number 2 because 12 is the second element of the range.

Errors

Quando scriviamo una funzione, l'errore è sempre dietro l'angolo, che sia di distrazione o per mancanza di conoscenza della funzione, Excel tende sempre ad avvisarci dell'errore commesso spiegandoci, nel suo linguaggio, che tipo di errore abbiamo commesso.

Caratteristica della segnalazione di errore in Excel, è una stringa preceduta dal simbolo # (cancelletto) seguito da una indicazione molto concisa dell'errore.

La seguente tabella riassume in maniera chiara e immediata quali siano i possibili errori che andiamo ad incontrare. Conoscerli è molto importante, soprattutto per poter comprendere in maniera immediata cosa si è sbagliato.

ERROR	MEANING

#NULL!	Refers to two areas that do not intersect
#DIV/0!	Division by zero
#VALUE!	The argument entered in the function is wrong or nonexistent
#RIF!	Cannot locate cells shown as range or reference
#NAME?	The name referred to is wrong or nonexistent
#NUM!	Misuse of a number within the function
#N/D	The function cannot find the requested value

Before closing the section pertaining to functions, I would like to say a few words about the importance of parentheses. You may have noticed that in the various examples all functions require them, and since Excel is a management-type software, precision is absolute. Therefore, especially when you happen to write more complex functions or functions with various search criteria, you must pay close attention to the use of parentheses

Excel makes our job easier by highlighting in different colors the various pairs of parentheses as they are typed, in case you come to a nesting of functions that would allow parenthesis paranthesis, Excel changes the color to the various pairs. This allows us to control one absolutely fundamental thing that many people do not give much thought to: when you open a parenthesis, you must close it. This is a fundamental law that we must keep well in mind, otherwise Excel will signal us the error. In these cases distraction is always around the corner, so before you think you have the wrong argument or function, always check the parentheses well.

Database in Excel

In the IT management of companies or Internet servers, databases and their functionality are becoming increasingly important. Their role is absolutely essential now for developing not only software, but for storing and searching data. Just think of search engines that are in fact huge databases encompassing data every day growing in importance.

Data are gaining in importance so much so that they have also become an economic asset so much so that a database also gains in importance based on the data it accommodates. The storage, selection and analysis of data that a database allows us are a mine of information that will become increasingly important in the near future. Therefore, understanding how they work and how they select data is absolutely essential.

But what really is a database?

A database refers to a structured collection of information, created for the purpose of being able to access, view and modify it either locally or on the network without having to worry about how it is stored.

The data contained in databases are organized in Tables, yes just like Excel tables, the rows that form these tables are called records while the columns are called fields.

Therefore, the strongest difference between any database and an Excel spreadsheet lies in the fact that records and fields in a table are not identified by cell code as might be A2 or C20, but can be accessed by indicating the name of the table, the name of a field, and a criterion (or filter) to select the records that are contained in that particular field.

An undoubted advantage of using Excel is its ability to interface with any database to take data from it and, if necessary, modify it within one's worksheet. This is no small advantage, especially for those who are unfamiliar with SQL (the programming language that is now standard when it comes to creating and managing databases) or with editing and entering data within a database.

In Figure 10.1 you can see the command that allows you to interface Excel to data from a database (or other external data source) so that you can not only download it but also possibly modify it.

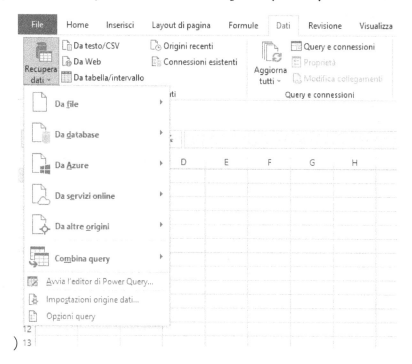

Figure 10.1 Data recovery from database

A little mention of Azure: Microsoft Azure is a cloud platform that offers a rich array of services and in particular managed database service. Through this platform, to give you an example, companies can manage services without needing a local infrastructure while saving money on it.

As you can see from the figure, the list of databases supported by Excel is extensive, and the procedure for retrieving data from them is automatic and intuitive. Even, you can retrieve data from an Internet site. We will have to discuss this later in the section devoted to Power Query.

It should be pointed out, however, that when dealing with a huge amount of data, Excel cannot be used as a database since there are real programs designed for this field.

If you have Excel on your computer you will certainly have the Office suite and with it the Microsoft Access program. Access is a database designed to store data and perform all the operations that any database requires. Access, unlike Excel which does not allow the construction and management of databases, is a database because it gives you the ability to create relationships between tables and to use QUERY, or query strings, to manage the data in the database.

What is an Excel database?

This question has already been answered above, but thinking about what a database is and what elements make it up, we can succinctly say that Excel databases are lists in which a list is nothing more than a table divided in turn into rows and columns. In the first row are written the column headings (which in database language we have discovered are the fields), the other rows, which contain an element of our list, are what are called records.

A simple and straightforward example of a database with Excel is, for example, a list of members of an association with membership number, full name, address, cell phone number and e-mail address.

Once we have created our database (or rather "list" in Excel terms) we can take advantage of some functions designed specifically to manage data in this way. These are precisely functions developed for working on databases and that are already distinguished in the callsign that begins, for all of them, with the letters DB (acronym for database) followed by the classic dot that we have already known in the section dedicated to functions and another keyword. Characteristic of these functions is the use of three arguments to identify any data on which the functions will work: the name of the database, the field (or column) and a criterion that allows the selection of data within our field of interest.

There are as many as twelve functions involved, and we can briefly get an idea of them by scrolling through and reading our table summarizing these types of functions.

FUNCTION	RESULT
DCOUNT	Count cells containing numbers
DCOUNTA	Counts cells containing data
DSTDEV	Delivers an estimate of the standard deviation based on a limited sample of the selected items
DSTDEVP	Delivers an estimate of the standard deviation based on all selected items
DVAR	Delivers an estimate of the variance based on a sample of selected items
DVARP	Delivers the variance based on all selected items
DMAX	Delivers the maximum value of the selected items
DAVERAGE	Performs the mean of the selected items
DMIN	Delivers the minimum value of the selected items
DPRODUCT	Multiplies the values in a given field of records that meet specific criteria

DSUM	Sums the values of a given field of records that meet specific criteria.
DGET	Count cells containing a data item.

DCOUNT()

The DCOUNT() function allows you to count all those cells that contain numbers within a field (column) of records in a list.

This is the syntax of the formula:

DCOUNT(database; field; criteria)

Where database is the range of cells that makes up our list of interest (or database); field indicates which column is used by the function while criteria is the range of cells containing the criteria that specify which records are to be included in the calculation.

DCOUNTA()

The DCOUNTA()function provides a count of the nonempty cells in a given field (or column) of records within a list (or database) that can satisfy the specified conditions.

The syntax of this formula is as follows:

DCOUNTA (database; field; criteria).

Database, of course, is the range of cells that make up our list under consideration. Field indicates the column that will be used by our function remembering to enter the column name in quotation marks. Criteria, on the other hand, is the range of cells containing the specified conditions.

DSTDEV()

The DSTDEV() function gives us the standard deviation based on a sample using the numbers in a field (or column) of records in a list that meet the specified conditions.

For those unfamiliar with statistics, it should be specified that the standard deviation of a variable is a kind of summary index of the differences in the values of each observation from the variable mean. In even simpler words it is the deviation, or distance, from the mean.

The syntax is as follows:

DSTDEV (database; range; criteria).

Database is the range of cells that make up our list under attention. Field indicates the column that will be used by our function remembering to enter the column name in quotation marks. Criteria, on the other hand, is the range of cells containing the specified conditions.

DSTDEVP()

The DSTDEVP() function gives us the standard deviation based on all selected entries using the numbers in a field (or column) of records in a list that meet the specified conditions.

DSTDEVP (database; field; criteria)

Database is the range of cells that make up our list that is the object of attention. Field indicates the column that will be used by our function remembering to enter the column name in quotation marks. Criteria, on the other hand, is the range of cells containing the specified conditions.

DVAR()

The DVAR() function allows us to calculate the variance based on a sample using the numbers of a field (or column) of records in a given element.

It is useful to specify that the variance is the dispersion of the values of a given variable around the mean value. The smaller the variance, the more concentrated the values our variable takes will be around the mean value.

This is the syntax:

DVAR(database; field; criteria)

Database is the range of cells that make up our list that is the object of attention. Field indicates the column that will be used by our function remembering to enter the column name in quotes. Criteria, on the other hand, is the range of cells containing the specified conditions.

DVARP()

The DVARP function allows us to calculate the variance based on all selected entries using the numbers of a field (or column) of records in a given element.

This is the syntax:

DVARP (database; field; criteria)

Database is the range of cells that make up our list object of attention. Field indicates the column that will be used by our function remembering to enter the column name in quotes. Criteria, on the other hand, is the range of cells containing the specified conditions.

DMAX()

THE DMAX function allows us to get the largest number of a given field (or column) of records in a specific list.

Here is the syntax:

DMAX(database; field; criteria)

Database is the range of cells that make up our list that is the object of attention. Field indicates the column that will be used by our function remembering to enter the column name in quotes. Criteria, on the other hand, is the range of cells containing the specified conditions.

DAVERAGE()

THE DAVERAGE() function allows us to obtain the average of the values of a specific field (or column) of records in a specific list.

Here is the syntax:

DAVERAGE (database; field; criteria)

Database is the range of cells that make up our list that is the object of attention. Field indicates the column that will be used by our function remembering to enter the column name in quotes. Criteria, on the other hand, is the range of cells containing the specified conditions.

DMIN()

THE DMIN function allows us to get the smallest number of a specific field (or column) of records in a specific list.

Here is the syntax:

DMIN(database; field; criteria)

Database is the range of cells that make up our list that is the object of attention. Field indicates the column that will be used by our function remembering to enter the column name in quotes. Criteria, on the other hand, is the range of cells containing the specified conditions.

DPRODUCT()

The function DPRODUCT allows us to be able to multiply the values of a field (or column) of records in a given database.

Here is the syntax:

DPRODUCT(database; field; criteria).

Database is the range of cells that make up our list that is the object of attention. Field indicates the column that will be used by our function remembering to put the column name in quotes. Criteria, on the other hand, is the range of cells containing the specified conditions.

It should be specified that any range can be used as the criteria argument as long as it has at least a column label, and a cell below the column label, in which the condition is specified.

DSUM()

The DSUM function allows us to sum values of a given range of records that can satisfy the specified criteria.

Here is the syntax:

DSUM(database; field; criteria)

Database is the range of cells that make up our list object of attention. *Field* indicates the column that will be used by our function remembering to enter the column name in quotation marks. Criteria, on the other hand, is the range of cells containing the specified conditions.

DGET()

The DGET() function allows the extraction of a single value found in a list or database that reflects the given conditions.

This is the syntax:

DGET (database; field; criteria)

Database is the range of cells that make up our list that is the object of attention. Field indicates the column that will be used by our function remembering to enter the column name in quotation marks. Criteria, on the other hand, is the range of cells containing the specified conditions.

Why use Excel database functions: advantages and disadvantages

As we had a chance to explain in the previous section, it is somewhat inaccurate to call Excel a database since the greatest disadvantage of this program is that you are limited to a single list, i.e., a single table, without being able to have relationships with other tables and without having the possibility of making QUERIES.

Let us briefly recall that in the database field the term QUERY is used to refer to a query of a database by a user, put even more simply a Query is nothing more than the word you type into the Google box to start your searches within the engine.

Having dutifully premised this, Excel's database functions undoubtedly have some advantages that cannot be overlooked and that, to some extent, have already emerged in our discussion of these functions in the previous section.

Undoubtedly they are on average simple to use and understand (provided you get into the logic of databases by understanding how these computer solutions reason), and no matter what function you want to use or need, you will have noticed that the three parameters that must be passed to the function always remain the same in all of them. This makes it significantly faster and smoother to write as well as easier to memorize.

A noticeable advantage is that they do not require any changes to update the results, as you were able to read in the previous paragraph you only need to change the criteria.

They allow us the use of logical operators such as AND or OR thus giving us the possibility of transforming them into filters, and thus any data selections within our tables or worksheets, much more complex than the appropriate Filter command.

The disadvantages we are going to encounter are essentially two: one related to the nature of Excel and the other to the functions.

In order to use the database functions we have to consider each and every table we are going to create as a real database, so even in construction and design. What does this mean in practical terms? That for example we will have to assign a name to the entire range occupied by our table or list.

The columns (or fields to use database language) will therefore have to be labeled in a way that uniquely identifies them to the individual fields, and each of these must contain data all of the same type. In a few simple words, the table we are going to create will have to be rigid and extremely detailed. Only by structuring the tables in this way will we be able to use Excel's database functions.

The other disadvantage is the functions. Although, as we wrote earlier, they are easily intuitable in their use, they do not have the power of a query, and the searches we can do are limited to the only twelve functions in Excel.

Given that Excel tables are used for a variety of topics, one could probably find oneself in the situation of having no purpose for using them. Therefore, already at the design stage, it should be addressed right away whether our table should be such or turn into a list (or database).

Pivot Tables

Introduction to Pivot Tables

More often than not, it happens that the information we need is extracted from a simple comparison of homogeneous data referring to different times or contexts: for example, it often happens that the sales departments of companies compare their sales results of a given period with that of the identical period but last year. When we find ourselves in the need to make such a comparison, the tool called a Pivot table proves to be decidedly convenient and useful.

I believe that never in this case it is appropriate to dwell on the name of this table since it can help to better understand its functionality and its being within Excel. Pivot is a term borrowed from sports, and in particular from basketball, by which we identify a player, particularly tall, on whom not only the entire game in its offensive phase but also the recovery of the ball in case it ends up bouncing on the game board goes to rest and revolve.

Now let us try to adapt that definition to a table.

A Pivot table allows us to arrange the data so that we can compare them with each other in groups, rotating a reference group from time to time just as Pivots do, so that it acts as a hinge and can be chosen from the various data in front of us. In fact we can consider the Pivot table as a kind of summary table.

The usefulness of this type of table comes from the fact that in businesses, the computer systems that are used for management are able to easily produce large amounts of data in raw format that can be obtained from their databases and thus made available to individual offices. Therefore, those who receive this data are faced with a mine of potential information that can only be extracted through the use of Pivot Tables, which allow us to select this data.

Creating a Pivot Table

Only by starting from a data range, or a structured table, can we begin to construct our Pivot table. It must be made clear right away that the construction of such a table is neither simple nor intuitive since the elements required for its composition are numerous and complex, so we need to understand well the characteristics of this Excel tool in order to be able to use and interpret it with regard to the data analysis part.

So let us try to begin with a very simple example, constructing a Pivot table in order to analyze the data shown in the table in Figure 11.1

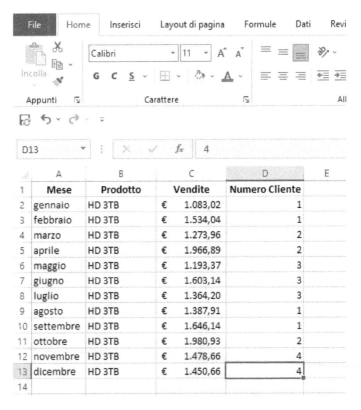

Figure 11.1 Tabella

When we set out to build a Pivot table, it is usually a good operating rule to organize the data by arranging the columns so that the first one on the left represents the first level of grouping (in our case the month), the next one on the right will be the second level of grouping (the product), and so on for other levels of grouping that may be of interest to us.

You are not, of course, obliged to organize your data in the way we have suggested also because this can be done through the layout of the Pivot table, but following a method allows you to see at a glance the possible correlation that may exist between the source data in the Pivot table. As well as help you in assimilating a powerful Excel tool like this that is not the easiest to understand.

Always remember that when we are dealing with data analysis, regardless of any Excel capabilities or commands, it is right to begin by structuring the data and values in a rigorous and precise manner. It may seem like a waste of time at first, but you will see that as your work provides you will realize that you have actually gained a lot of time.

A small and necessary note: the source table for our data can have fields that contain calculated values, i.e., formulas, but it absolutely must not have fields with column totals that will have to be eliminated.

In constructing this type of table, it is considered a convenience, along with a fair way to begin designing it, to assign a name to the entire table and any ranges identified by individual columns (you remember, don't you, what was written in database functions?). To be able to accomplish this we will simply select our table, including the column labels, move to our ribbon and give the command Formulas/Name Management/Create from Selection.

Now we need to start organizing this in the form of a Pivot table. Let us position ourselves as usual in our ribbon and type Insert/Pivot Table getting what we can see in the window in figure 11.2.

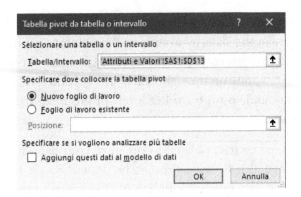

Figure 11.2 Create Pivot Table

As can be safely inferred from the window, we are asked to indicate where our data is located by specifying where to place our table giving us only two options.

Once we set the data as in our example figure, we will be placed within a new Excel sheet where what is formally called the Pivot table report will be placed where, within the ribbon, a new tab named Pivot table tools will be visible.

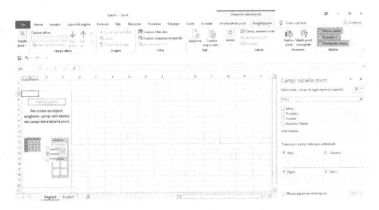

Figure 11.3 Pivot table ratio

In the window on the right, called Pivot Table Fields and where we can add the fields we are interested in for the report, we find a cogwheel icon. Clicking on it brings up a view of the following window in Figure 11.4.

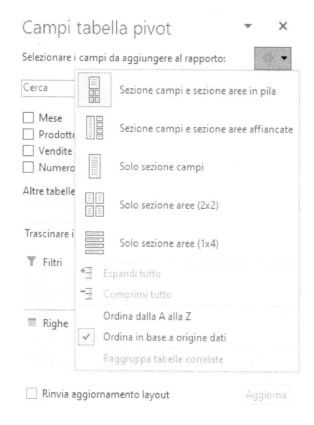

Figure 11.4 Table configuration

The window in Figure 11.4 is a tentative start to modifying the layout of a Pivot table, which will be discussed in more detail in the next section. Suffice it to say that the first section, the one called the fields and areas section in the stack, is the one used by default. Over time, and depending on your project and what data to focus on, you will gradually find what you think will be the best configuration for your Pivot table.

Let us now return to the Pivot Table Fields window. As you can see the names that appear would be those of the columns, which are called fields here as we have already seen when we wrote about database functions in Excel.

It is not obligatory to select all the fields, remember that the Pivot table is in fact a summary table; therefore, only those fields should be selected that are essential for us and that allow us to better understand the relationships between values and data sets.

Below the list we can see four squares in which you can drag the field names. If we try to approach the cursor by pointing it with our mouse it becomes a cross.

- Columns will form the table headers;
- row will form the row headers;
- values will see the entry of fields that correspond to columns of numeric values automatically creating a summation;
- filter will have within it the field corresponding to the most generic data column.

Lastly you will find the Postpone Layout Update box; if the checkbox has a check mark, the Pivot table will be generated only when the Update button next to it is pressed.

Figure 11.5 shows the Pivot table obtained through our example.

Figure 11.5 Tabella Pivot

Formatting and Layout of a Pivot Table

We have already seen in Figure 11.4 how we can already act at the level of layout formation in our Pivot table.

Keeping our example Pivot table still, the middle part contains the values contained in the sales column of the source table, broken down by customer number.

The values corresponding to sales are summed at the bottom of each row and column.

If we wanted, we could have organized the data in our source table in this same way with the help of the commands we have already seen: Copy, Paste special and with the SUM() function. In doing so, however, we would have obtained only a static table with the disadvantage of having to rearrange the data whenever we wanted to examine a different combination of them.

The Pivot table, thanks to the aggregation elements we have seen in the Filters, Columns, Rows and Values areas, allows us to select the values to be displayed, thus expanding the numbers of rows and columns to be presented in the central pane.

Herein lies the real hinge of Pivot tables, these in fact are the real ideal pivots around which the data are rotated. Precisely, as we mentioned earlier, does the Pivot player during the game.

Once we have completed and organized our Pivot table we can, like any Excel table, change or improve the formatting and layout. To do this, once we have selected our table, we need the commands that will emerge from the ribbon with the name Pivot table tools. Figures 11.6 and 11.7 show us entirely the related commands on this tab.

Figure 11.6 Pivot table analysis

Figure 11.7 Pivot Table Design

From Figure 11.6 we will mention the most popular and usually most heavily used commands allowing us to work directly on the data in the Pivot table.

Insert Data Filter allows us to use a filter of the data in order to visually select it. Beyond data allows us to filter tables, Pivot tables, Pivot charts (which we will have do to see later) and cube functions that we will go into more detail in the chapter on Excel advanced level.

Insert Time Sequence allows us to be able to use a time sequence to filter data interactively. This command also allows us to filter tables, Pivot tables, Pivot charts, and cube functions.

Refresh is a command you might use frequently. It allows us, should we change the value of a data item in the source table, to find it immediately updated in our Pivot table. In the Update All version, it will update all cell data.

Change data source allows the replacement of the original data with data from another table or sequence of cells. It is useful, in the case of two tables, to get an idea of different variations with different source data.

Actions allows deleting, moving or selecting our Pivot table.

Pivot Chart allows us the creation of a chart of our choice inherent to our Pivot table.

In the series of commands inherent to the design of the Pivot table, we are going to give a kind of artist's touch to our table. A touch that will enhance our glance at the data by allowing us to see relationships or inconsistencies at a glance.

Subtotals and Totals allows us to see or hide rows containing totals or subtotals.

Layout Report allows us to change the layout of our report.

Blank Rows allows the addition of blank rows between each grouped item helping to improve readability.

Quick Pivot Table Styles to put colorful, alternating row highlighting of the table depending on the color we choose.

Dynamic data analysis with Pivot tables.

In order to fully appreciate the functionality of a Pivot table, it is a good idea to work with a source table, i.e., the first table containing all our data, that contains a good amount of data, including at least one column (or field) of dates. Always keep in mind what the Pivot athlete does and how he plays.

Grouping of Pivot Table elements.

Manual grouping

To manually group data, we will simply select the range of cells we are interested in (highlight the first cell and then click on the last cell while holding down the SHIFT key if the range is contiguous; press CTRL and select individual cells if the range is not contiguous). Now just right-click to see the menu in Figure 11.8.

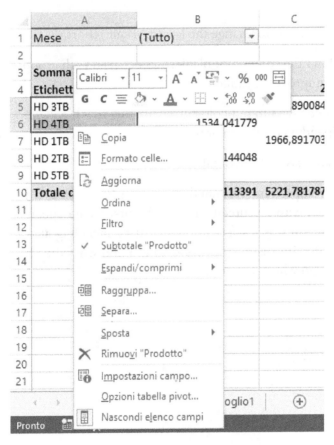

Figure 11.8 menù

If, on the other hand, we want to undo our previous command and thus untie the cells we have grouped, we need only select the Separate command.

Automatic grouping of fields containing dates

Grouping by date is perhaps one of the most interesting functions that Pivot tables provide along with one of the most interesting in selecting data representing this type of table.

Many times, especially in tables that curate and collect attendance or warehouse management, there is almost daily data entry that, while very useful, can be too detailed.

Let us try, for example, to imagine that we are interested in data aggregation on a monthly basis. How can we do this? In organizing our Pivot table, we will simply place the field (or column) containing the dates in the area called row. We will then get in our Pivot table the column containing all the dates that we can already select by clicking on the triangle icon to activate the filter.

What we wish to have, however, is a grouping by month, so we will position ourselves on any date in our column and right-click and choose the Group command that we have seen before. Excel will recognize the presence of dates and propose automatic grouping, these will also allow us to be able to see the most current date, and the least current date, among the several that appear in the database.

To view the situation by quarter or perhaps by quarter and month, simply place yourself in the grouping window and also select Quarters or deselect Quarters and select Months. If the table has time references for more than one year, you can also group on an annual basis.

Automatic grouping of fields containing numbers (creating a frequency distribution).

Grouping of numbers is referred to as frequency distribution. What it means. It means that all values are divided into homogeneous classes, and our Pivot table performs the calculation not on the individual values but on the classes.

Assuming a refresher course for a particular job, knowing the age of the participants, we proceeded to create a Pivot table that counts the number of participants according to their age of birth.

The age was entered in the Row Labels and the course name in the Values area. Now our requirement is to collect the ages in 3 bands (20-29, 20-29, and 40-49) or in 6 bands (20-24, 25-29, 30-34, 35-39, 40-44, 45-49) to produce a frequency distribution.

As with chronological grouping, one must right-click on any age among those in the Pivot, then click on the Group command. Excel again detects automatic grouping due to the presence of numerical values and indicates the minimum value (from) and the maximum value (up to). In the Grouping section, we need to identify the grouping criterion i.e. every 10 (20-29 etc.) or every 5 (20-24).

The only catch is that the frequency classes must be similar, i.e., to stay in the context of our example, you cannot mix a grouping of 5 with one of 10 (20-29, 30-34).

By doing this, our Pivot table will show us the number of training participants based on the age range we requested.

Sorting and filtering data

Sorting data in a Pivot table.

To sort our data within a Pivot table we have, in a nutshell, two viable paths. The first is to select any cell within our Pivot table containing one of the values we need to sort. Once selected, all we need to do is right-click and we can see the result of the operation as in window 11.9.

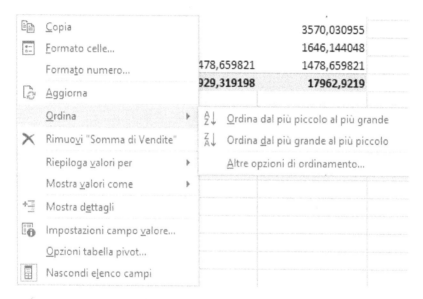

Figure 11.9 Sorting Pivot Table Values

Here we find two commands that we already learned about when we wrote about how to sort our table data.

Sort from smallest to largest allows us to distribute our values in ascending order, that is, from smallest to largest value. If they are string they will be distributed in alphabetical order from A to Z.

Sort from largest to smallest allows us to distribute our values in descending order, that is, from the largest value to the smallest value. If, however, they were to be strings they will be distributed in reverse alphabetical order, that is, from Z to A.

Other sorting options allow us to open and display the window in Figure 11.10.

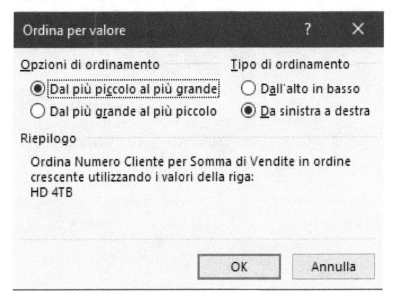

Figure 11.10 Other sorting options

The second way, which we already learned about while talking about sorting data in a table, is to select the Data tab within our ribbon and then select the Sort command within the Sort and Filter section.

Filtering Pivot Tables with the ratio filter and the data filter.

The ratio filter allows us to have a unique distribution of our data, based on the field of our interest, along the time distribution creating, depending on each time interval, a table in each worksheet.

To achieve this, we need to select our Pivot table and, within Pivot Table Tools, choose Pivot Table Analysis by positioning ourselves on the Pivot Table command located on the far left, here we choose Options and click on Show Report Filter Pages.

Figure 11.10 Filter ratio

Once we select Show report filter pages, the window depicted in figure 11.11 will appear.

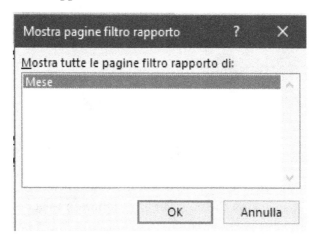

Figure 11.11 report filter pages

We select the field we are interested in, in our example it is Month, and after clicking the ok button, in the toolbar, the one at the bottom of the worksheet, where there are tabs identifying the name of our worksheets, there will appear, in our case, the tabs with the names of the months inside which will be the summary table inherent to the month we are interested in.

The data filter, on the other hand, works like this:after we have positioned ourselves on the Pivot Table Tools tab, we select the

Insert Data Filter command to obtain, as in figure 11.12, a window containing the fields we are interested in filtering.

Figure 11.12 Data filter

Once we have selected the field we are interested in filtering, or fields, we need only click on the now familiar ok button to get our filter as displayed by the figure below.

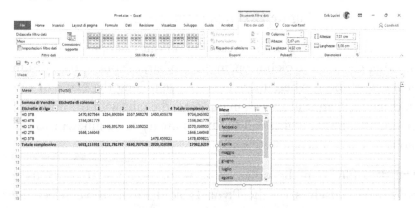

Figure 11.13 Final data filter

After selecting the field of our interest, or fields, our window containing the filter will appear next to the table. Clicking on each individual entry will cause our Pivot table to display only the rows of our interest based on what we have selected, hiding, of course, the other rows that will not be of interest to us and that do not fall within our selection. In our example it will be by month.

A key feature of this filter is that once activated it gives rise to a new tab called Data Filter where we can perform certain and various operations. First, we can change the size of our window containing the filter. We can change the style of our filter by varying the colors to achieve better readability of our data. We can, a powerful and important command, change the settings of our filter.

To do this we need only select the Data Filter Settings command located at the top of our ribbon to get the following window of options.

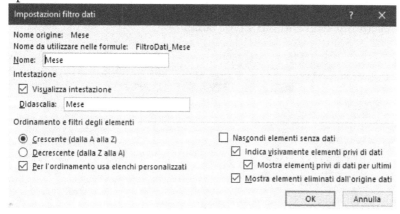

Figure 11.14 Data filter options

We will not dwell on the options contained in this window since on the one hand they are easily guessed and on the other hand we have already learned about them by talking about data sorting.

It remains always to keep in mind, in this case more than in others, the great power of Excel also with regard to configurations and settings that make its filters as adaptable as if they were tailor-made clothes.

Our advice is to experiment with the filters several times, even if at first you will have tables with little data and it will seem useless, but in fact you will soon realize their essentiality and not only as far as the Pivot table is concerned, but for the spreadsheet in general.

Creating a Pivot Chart

Pivot tables have their own set of graphical tools that makes it extremely easy to create and display a graph of the data in them.

To do this, simply select our Pivot table, locate on the Pivot Table Tools tab, choose Pivot Table Analysis, and click on the Pivot Chart command located on the far right of our ribbon bar.

When this is done, the following window will materialize before our eyes, allowing us to choose the chart we think is most suitable to represent our data and our Pivot table.

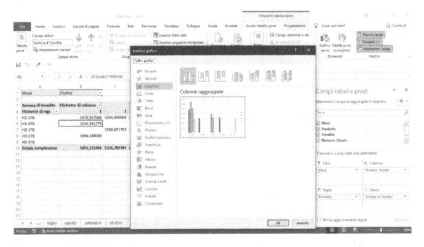

Figure 11.15 Pivot Chart

Once we have chosen our chart, we need only click the ok button for the chart of our choice to be immediately displayed.

Selecting the chart will display a new tab within our ribbon called Pivot Chart Tools which will be divided into three sub tabs called Pivot Chart Analysis, Design and Format.

Through these sub tabs you will be able to edit every single part of our chart. We will not dwell on it since the commands you will see we have already learned about in other areas, but it is still worth emphasizing the extraordinary power and pliability of a tool like Pivot Charts in which Excel gives us complete freedom in being able to edit each and every element.

Even in the case of the Pivot table Excel shows its great pliability in the field of graphical representation of values. Outside of what may be our preferences when it comes to graphs, let us always remember that it is nothing more than a tool for displaying our data; therefore, we must be shrewd and certain in its choice relying solely on what we believe to be the best to depict our table and our values in general.

As we have already mentioned talking about charts in the relevant chapter, each of them has peculiarities that help us to better enhance the relationships we want to highlight from the analysis of our data.

Unfortunately, perfection is not of this world and, some limitations pivot charts have. We would be sinning in presumption if we did not mention these as well. However, it must be said that for the average user they are issues that do not affect their work in the slightest.

As we have already acquired by now, pivot tables allow the user to use a single table of source data. This is fine for very simple datasets with few fields and from which we need to extract very simple information, but as our project grows, and with it our cognitive ambitions of what may lie behind the relationships in our data, it very quickly becomes a limitation.

As a rule, it is very common for source data to be split into multiple tables, particularly if you get your data from a database program (as we have written about before, a database works on the principle of relationships between multiple tables). If the data are split into different tables, it becomes arduous to use pivot tables. In addition (and more recently with the advent of cloud computing and social networks) people acquire data in different places and want to compare these data as one.

The Excel user must then use VLOOKUP (or similar) to bring the data into a single table before a pivot table can be created. We can therefore understand how this ends up being a problem for performance, configuration work, and maintenance effort.

Always keep in mind that Excel can only store 1 million rows of data; therefore, we can overlook the idea of trying to use pivot tables on very large data sets. (Actually, it is possible to connect standard pivot tables to an Analysis Services data cube, but this requires an expensive IT infrastructure and effort to create and maintain, so it is not considered feasible for the average Excel user.)

Well before you reach the 1 million row limit, Excel will start to perform very poorly, particularly if you have many VLOOKUPs etc. Excel is not optimized for large database processing work.

So, to use an extreme summary, pivot tables are great for visualization, as long as the data is optimized to take advantage of the power of pivot tables.

Is there a way to be able to curb these limitations? Yes, and it will be covered in a future chapter devoted to Power Pivot.

Excel Livello Avanzato

Power Query

Power Query is a business intelligence tool, i.e., a set of business processes for collecting data and analyzing strategic information, available in Excel that allows data to be imported from different sources and then cleaned, transformed, and reshaped as needed.

To better understand what Power Query is, it is important to say a few words about business intelligence to which, fundamentally, we owe the emergence of tools such as precisely power query and power Pivot.

Business intelligence combines business analysis, data mining, data visualization, data tools and infrastructure, and best practices to help organizations make decisions that are more data-driven. In practice, you know you have modern business intelligence when you have a complete view of your organization or company's data and use it to drive change, eliminate inefficiencies, and adapt quickly to market or supply changes.

Traditional business intelligence, capital letters and all, originally emerged in the 1960s as a system for sharing information among organizations. It developed further in the 1980s along with computer models for decision making and turning data into detailed information before becoming a specific offering of BI teams (short for Business Intelligence) with IT-based service solutions.

In light of what we have learned inherent to Business Intelligence, we can already have an idea of the extraordinary usefulness of a tool like Power Query.

Power Query is a self-service ETL (Extract, Transform, Load) tool that functions as an add-on to Excel. It allows users to extract data from a variety of sources, manipulate the data specified in a form that matches their needs, and load it into Excel.

<u>In a nutshell, Power Query allows the following operations:</u>

- Download data in Excel from nearly 40 different sources, including databases such as SQL, Oracle, Access, Teradata, enterprise ERP systems such as SAP, Microsoft Dynamics, Internet services such as Facebook, Google Analytics, and almost any site.
- Collect data from files of all basic data types such as XLSX, TXT, CSV, JSON, HTML, either individually or in bulk, from all files in the specified folder. From Excel workbooks, you can automatically download data from all sheets at the same time.
- Delete data defined as "junk": extra columns or rows, repetitions, service information in the "header," extra spaces or unprintable characters, etc.
- Put data in order: correct upper and lower case, number as text, fill in the blanks, add the correct table header, disassemble text that sticks to columns and join it again, split data into components, etc.
- Transform tables in any way by developing them into the desired view (filter, sort, change column order, transpose, sum totals, expand cross tables into flat tables, and restore).
- Replace data from one table to another by the coincidence of one or more parameters, i.e., perfectly replace the VPR function (VLOOKUP) and its analogs.

As a corollary to what has been written so far and despite the strength and complexity of this tool, Power Query does not require learning specific code. This is, undoubtedly, a major advantage for learning the tool, which is faster that way.

Power Query is the most powerful data automation tool found in Excel. It allows a user to import data into Excel via external sources such as text files, CSV files, Web or Excel workbooks, to list just a few. Data can then be "cleaned," prepared and selected for our needs.

Power Query includes several useful built-in features, such as adding data and creating relationships between different data sets. This is called data set merging. We can also group and summarize data with the help of the tool. Needless to say, it is a very useful tool.

It also eliminates the need to perform the same filtering techniques to transform the same dataset at different times; the user only needs to set up a query, i.e., the rules for sorting, once, and update the query each time the action needs to be repeated.

Power Query is programmed to export data from a variety of sources, including but not limited to text files, Excel workbooks, and CSV files.

When additions to the same source data must be imported at regular time intervals, such as every week or every month, it becomes difficult to manually ensure that the data are replicated correctly.

Power Query offers the ability to combine different data sets. Sales reports for each month can be combined with that of previous months by specifying the necessary instructions.

Once set up, a query is stored in the system, and each time data needs to be imported and formatted similarly, the instructions can be repeated using the update option. It eliminates the need for repetitive manual work and makes the process more efficient.

It allows you to establish a query once and then employ it with a fairly simple update. It is also quite powerful. Power Query can import and clean up millions of rows in the data model for later analysis. The user interface is quite intuitive and is done well, therefore, it is easy to use. It is a fairly short learning curve compared to other Excel tools such as formulas or VBA (short for Visual Basic for Application). The best part is that you do not have to learn or use any code to do any of it.

The Power Query commands are located within the Data tab and are the fetch and transform data and Queries and connections panes

To begin working with Power Query we need to move from the range to the table. To do this we will simply select any box inherent to the range of our data and click the from table/interval command found on the Data tab of the ribbon.

Here a window will appear telling us the range of our data, usually Excel can identify all of them, if by chance some box is missing, you can enter it manually. After pressing ok the Power Query window will appear as in figure 12.1.

Note that the automatically formed column labels represent the type of data in it.

Figure 12.1 Power Query

Now, the extraordinary advantage of Por Query is that it allows us to do even simple things with just a few clicks. Assume, for example, that we want to remove duplicates (i.e., all those values that repeat) from the product column. Normally in Excel we would have to, as you know, sort the data and then remove those that are duplicates or, alternatively, have to use a long and complex function. With Power Query, on the other hand, we can solve this in just a few steps.

First we position ourselves in the column where we want to find the duplicate values, in our example it is the product column. Here, using the right mouse button we select remove other columns so we can isolate our column of interest. Next, we sort our values by clicking on the triangle icon located to the right of the label and, again using the right mouse button select the remove duplicates item.

All in a few simple steps. This is what the power of a tool like Power Query is all about.

To get an idea of it, just look at the applied steps pane of query setup positioned on the right. There you will see in order the steps you have taken, and clicking on one of them will immediately take you back to the time when you selected the step.

Power Query, as we have already written, allows you to use it without knowing the Visual Basic Application (VBA) language, but that doesn't mean you don't use it. Let's try selecting the View tab and then clicking on Advanced Editor. You will see the following window in Figure 12.2

Figure 12.2 Advanced Editor.

Excel, true to its principle of high configurability, allows thanks to this editor to intervene directly in the modification of the code, provided, of course, that you know VBA well.

Once we have finished our project, let us position ourselves on the close and load command inside the Home tab on the far left. Here we will return to our Excel sheet with the result obtained from Power Query as in Figure 12.3

Figure 12.3 Result on Excel sheet

Returning to our Excel sheet will bring up two new tabs: Table Tools and Query Tools that will allow us to modify the layout of the table and our query to our liking.

You will recall how when we wrote about databases we pointed out that Excel could not and is not a database partly because it was not able, which databases starting with Microsoft Access do, to create relationships between tables.

Power Query, thanks to the combine query command, tries to get closer. I repeat: come close, and that does not make Excel a database. Let us, before we conclude this chapter take a quick look at this interesting and important command. In order to activate it we will have to position ourselves in our ribbon, select the Data tab and, within it, select the Combine Query command that we find within the Retrieve Data command at the beginning of the tab.

Combine Query has two options: Merge and Add.

In Power Query, the Add operation creates a new table by joining all the rows of the first query, followed by all the rows of the second query. Follow the steps below to understand how to perform a queuing operation.

The Merge option, on the other hand, is similar to the JOIN function in SQL. Merge is a way to combine two existing queries and create a new query.

Power Query, as we have tried to demonstrate in this chapter, is a very versatile and powerful tool that we wanted to give you a taste of. Obviously, the larger and more complex the data, the greater the benefits of using Power Query.

To talk about it fully and comprehensively would require a separate text, but if you have some time on your hands, we highly recommend that you delve into this extraordinary Excel tool.

Power Pivot

Power Pivot is, like Power Query. An Excel add-on that allows us to perform effective data analysis and create sophisticated data models. With Power Pivot it is possible to merge high volumes of data from different sources, to perform information analysis completely quickly, and to share it seamlessly.

In both Excel and Power Pivot you can create a data model, a collection of tables with relationships. The data model represented in a workbook in Excel is the same data model that you can view in the Power Pivot window. Data that are imported into Excel are available in Power Pivot and vice versa.

As an illustration of the volumes of data that Power Pivot can move and analyze, suffice it to say that it can handle up to 300 million rows of raw data. Excel 2019 can handle up to a maximum of 1,048,576 rows. This power is also due to the powerful DAX formula language.

This rich formula language offers more powerful calculations than worksheet formulas in Excel and many more options than stand-alone pivot tables.

DAX stands for Data Analysis Expressions and is the formula language behind Power Pivot. It is a very rich language; there are many formulas and it is constantly evolving. There are two types of DAX formulae; measures and calculated columns.

Power Pivot is in fact a data analysis engine and, as in a virtual relay race, takes the place of Power Query which, as we have already seen, allows us to take data from external sources and modify it. Power Pivot models the data in order to be able to perform all the calculations on it to allow us an increasingly precise analysis of the data.

A pivot table is therefore a visualization tool that can aggregate data from a data source (historically a single table of Excel data) and display that data in a way that helps the reader make sense of the data. Figure 13. 1 shows us the Power Pivot tab within our multifunction bar

Figure 13.1 power Pivot menu

If by chance this tab does not appear for you, no problem. Click on File, Accounts, and then Options. In the Excel Options window that opens, select Data and then put a check mark in the Enable Data Analysis add-ons row: Power Pivot, Power View, and 3D Maps.

Now your Power Pivot tab will appear last in your ribbon.

Now let's go and select the Manage command to start Power Pivot. Power Pivot is an analysis engine and is structured to manage an OLAP cube. We will look at the OlAP cube in more detail in the next section.

Figure 13.2 shows us the Power Pivot editor.

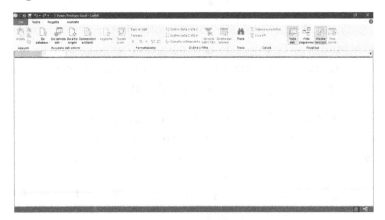

Figure 13.2 Power Pivot editor

Through this editor that creates three new tabs in its ribbon: Home, Design and Advanced we will be able to capture data, create our Power Pivot table and work on its layout. Warning: Power Pivot does not modify the data in any way, if you want to make such an option, as we have already seen, you will have to use Power Query.

Also keep in mind that Power Pivot is a tool that compresses the data, since it is not a relational-type database as Microsoft Access is, for example. Power Pivot therefore uses an engine called OLAP, which makes it a tool for an experienced data analysis user since this engine can handle a data range from 100 GB to Terabytes.

It goes without saying that Power Pivot is a tool suitable for handling huge volumes of data, but even in the case of a few it can have its extraordinary usefulness due to its data compression capacity that reaches about 34/35 times that of the data exposed in Excel.

Let us try, now, to create our first table with power Pivot. The first thing to keep well in mind is that power Pivot does not rely directly on a range of cells as is the case, and we have already seen in the dedicated section, with Pivot tables. Power Pivot relies on adding to a data model, which is that whole area of work where you can import data from Excel spreadsheets, external files or even databases.

So to add a range of cells to the data model, you simply open the Excel sheet where your Pivot table resides and there, selecting the Power Pivot tab click on the add to data model command in the tables pane.

Figure 13.3 shows you your first Power Pivot.

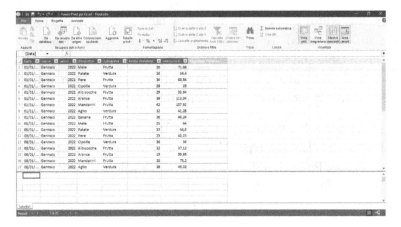

Figure 13.3 Power Pivot

You may have noticed that, from a formal and visual point of view, nothing has changed from our Pivot table. This is because, as we have written before, the novelty of this tool, and also its real power, lies in the fact that it relies on a database that offers us extraordinary data analysis scenarios.

While already this type of data analysis shows its efficiency and thanks to being able to allow relationships between multiple tables that power Pivot shows its full power. It is not for nothing that the name "power" refers to this very feature.

To create relationships between tables, we must keep in mind some simple rules that will help us in creating them: the first is that the eventual relationship can only be based on a single field (remember? Excel is not a database). The second is that the fields that will have a relationship must be of the same type. Finally, the third, the relationship is one-to-many, where one of the two tables must have as a key without copies, the field that is the subject of the relationship. Be very careful at this point, because if both tables have duplicate values, the data model management engine will reject the creation of the relation, sending back an error.

Held what has been written, let us operate directly on the tables by clicking on diagram view on the far right of our menu bar, to get the view in Figure 13.4

Figure 13.4 Power Pivot reports

At this point, always keeping in mind the rules written earlier, all we have to do is, with the help of the mouse, click on one field and move it to the other. You will immediately see a black line joining the die fields creating what we have just called a relationship.

After we have finished outlining and identifying the relationships we are interested in, we will just create our Pivot table, which, as we will see, will have something different this time: in the list of fields, we will see all the tables in the model, and by expanding them, the list of fields in each one will appear. There is therefore the possibility of summarizing data originating from multiple tables. The full power of power Pivot begins to unfold.

We can now deduce somewhat what some general principles for working in Power Pivot might be:

- First, load data into Power Pivot: which can support as many as 15 different computer sources: common databases (SQL, Oracle, Access...), Excel files, text files, data feeds. In addition, we can use

Power Query as a data source, which makes the analysis almost omnivorous and all-encompassing.

- Links are configured between loaded tables or, as they say, the Data Model is created, a technical term for what is called, in the engineering field, data modeling-that is, the process of creating a data model for a given information system. This will make it possible in the future to bring to life reports on any field in existing tables as if it were a single table.

- If necessary, further calculations are added to the data model with the help of calculated columns (by this term we identify a similar column with formulas present in an intelligent table) and measures (by this term, on the other hand, we identify a summarized calculated field). All this, let us remember, is written in a special DAX internal language (Data Analysis eXpressions).

The reports of interest to us in the form of pivot tables and charts are built on the Data Model Excel sheet. Power Pivot has several features that make it a unique tool for certain tasks

- In Power Pivot there is no limit to the number of rows (as in Excel). You can load tables of any size and work with them at your leisure.
- Power Pivot is very good at compressing data as it is loaded into the model. A 50 MB source text file can easily turn into 3-5 MB after downloading.
- For hidden in Power Pivot is, in effect, a full-fledged database engine capable of handling large amounts of information very quickly. We could even get as far as analyzing 10 to 15 million records used an old laptop.

Let us now draw a kind of summary and conclusion of this extraordinary tool.

As you may have already guessed, Power Pivot is a tool that allows you to prepare your data in a way that can be used by pivot tables.

Power Pivot is actually a data modeling tool. Power Pivot allows you to perform the following operations.

1.   Takes data from one or more computer sources and combines them together into a single data source (this is called a data model);

2.   It enhances the underlying data so that we can create new concepts derived from the data. So, for example, if we have Sales and Costs in our source data, we can create Sales Margins and Cost Margins and make these new concepts available for a pivot table.

3.   The new concepts we create in Power Pivot are infinitely reusable in our pivot tables. In traditional Excel we need to create formulas in individual cells by pointing to other source cells. If we want to reuse a formula we created on another sheet that is not identical in total to the first sheet, we actually have to rewrite the formula. This is not the case in Power Pivot. Instead, here we write the formula once in the data model, and this allows us to reuse it over and over again in as many pivot tables as we wish.

4.   Power Pivot compresses the source data and stores it as a database within the Excel workbook. This means that you can store 10 (even 100) of millions of rows of data directly in an Excel workbook in a highly compressed and performant way and distribute it to other people without them having to have access to the source database.

So Power Pivot is not a super Pivot table because Power Pivot does not change the functionality of pivot tables. What Power Pivot does do is modify the source data so that you can use data that could not be used previously and get much more out of the previously used data within a pivot table.

As with Power Query, Power Pivot would need a separate book and our disinterested advice is to, time permitting, approach it in more depth. The interplay of these two outstanding Excel features allows you remarkable data analysis not only quantitatively but especially qualitatively

OLAP cube

What is an OLAP cube?

OLAP stands for online analytical processing, and cube is another word for a multidimensional set of data; thus, an OLAP cube is a temporary management space for information analysis. Basically, a cube is a mechanism used to query data in organized dimensional structures for analysis.

An OLAP cube takes a spreadsheet-like structure and three-dimensionalizes analysis experiences. By breaking it down, OLAP means analytical rather than transactional data, and the cube part of the nomenclature refers to the storage aspect.

OLAP cubes are basically multidimensional databases. They store data for analysis, and many classic Business Inteligence products rely on OLAP cubes to access business information for reports, budgets or dashboards. For example, a CFO (chief financial officer) might want to generate reports on the company's financial data by location, by month, or by product-these elements would make up the size of this cube. However, OLAP cubes are not SQL Server relational databases, as are data warehouses.

With the OLAP cube, we move from data analysis to data structuring; the OLAP cube, which we mentioned in the previous section, is the technical reason that allows power Pivot to succeed in handling nearly 300 million rows of raw data. But how does it manage to do this?

Basically, the OLAP cube creates a compressed data in multiple dimensions by aggregating the measures based on the levels and hierarchies of each dimension we want to analyze, i.e., combine multiple dimensions. In practice there is a possibility that the cube can also become a hypercube. An OLAP dimension assumes the highest level in the structure of the OLAP data cube. It is the metadata element, which describes the key economic indicators of the enterprise's activity, e.g., products, customers, sales area and time period, etc.

OLAP dimensions help in grouping and filtering data for various reasons. Then this information can be detailed in other hierarchies, and this is how you can get an in-depth analysis of business data. Cubes are not cubes in the mathematical sense of the word because they do not have a geometric feature that the cube requires, namely, equal side lengths. In the OLAP cube, it is possible that the sides are not all equal

An OLAP cube does not have to cycle through any transactions because the totals are all precomputed, providing instant access. An OLAP cube is a snapshot of the data at a specific time, perhaps at the end of a specific day, week, month, or year.

When we create an OLAP Pivot table (power Pivot), from a data model, an OLAP cube is automatically created in computer memory. And it is used to power an OLAP Pivot table. An OLAP cube can be updated at any time, using the current values in the source tables. With very large data sets, Excel's reconstruction of the cube may take a long time.

Arranging data in cubes overcomes a limitation of relational databases, which are not suitable for near-instantaneous analysis and visualization of large amounts of data. Instead, they are better suited for creating records from a series of transactions known as OLTP or On-Line Transaction Processing. Although there are many report-writing tools for relational databases, these are slow when it is necessary to summarize the entire database and present great difficulty when users wish to reorient reports or analysis according to different multidimensional perspectives, aka Slices. The use of cubes facilitates this type of rapid end-user interaction with data.

Other operations besides Pivot tables can be applied to the OLAP cube. The most commonly used ones are drill-up, drill-down and slice-and-dice. Let us see, very briefly, what these are:

Drill up: this operation, also called OLAP cube roll up, involves collecting all obtainable data and calculating everything in one or more dimensions. Often this may require the use of a mathematical formula. As an OLAP example, we can examine a retail network with outlets scattered across several cities.

To identify patterns and anticipate future sales trends, data on them from all points are "rolled up" in the company's main sales department for consolidation and settlement.

Drill down: the drill down of the OLAP cube is the opposite of the drill up. The process begins with a large data set; then, it is broken down into smaller parts, allowing users to see the details. In the retail network example, the analyst will evaluate the sales data and examine the individual products rated as best at each store.

Slice and say: OLAP cube slice and say is a process in which analytical operations involve two actions: producing a specific dataset from a cube (the "slicing" aspect of the analysis) and viewing it from different viewpoints or angles. This can occur when all data outlets are captured and inserted into the hypercube. The analyst cuts a set of sales data from the OLAP cube. It will also show up in the analysis of individual unit sales in each region. At the same time, other users can focus on evaluating the cost-effectiveness of sales or the effectiveness of a marketing and advertising campaign.

In addition, there are many additional tools such as nesting, merging, and OLAP cube reader for visualization.

An OLAP cube can be thought of as an extension of the modeling structure provided by a spreadsheet, housing data in rows and columns, i.e., a two-dimensional array of data. A cube can accommodate any number of arrays or dimensions, although OLAP cube designers will try to create models that balance the needs of the user and the limitations of the logic model.

Two of the key essential elements of the OLAP cube architecture are:

1.   Data aggregation. This aggregation is often performed as a nightly process, especially if an OLAP cube is very large;
2.   Different data sets (sales, general ledger, inventory, accounts receivable, accounts payable, and so on) require a separate OLAP cube because all the data in one cube must be correlated so that they can be aggregated.

Because OLAP cubes are not a data warehouse (a data warehouse is nothing more than a database with special functions such as aggregation for data analysis)) of open SQL server, they require someone with the knowledge and experience to maintain them using a modeling language called MDX, whereas a SQL server data warehouse can be managed by most IT staff who have regular database training.

This aspect has a distinctly high cost as a result. A company needs to allocate time and energy from a current employee or consultant to focus on OLAP cube management or hire a new employee, perhaps full-time.

In addition, OLAP cubes tend to be more rigid and limited when it comes to designing reports because of their table-like functionality.

Aesthetics and capabilities could and probably should be important to a company that is building its portfolio of business intelligence solutions.

As with any tool, the OLAP cube has its pros and cons.

When the OLAP cube concept was first introduced in the 1990s, it was praised for being able to query a large amount of data in much less time than a data warehouse requires because the data is always aggregated into a cube.

OLAP cubes were also highly praised for having more intuitive user interfaces than first-generation data warehouses and for easily handling complex calculations. An OLAP cube gave companies detailed information about the inner workings of their business, allowing them to see the "how" and "why" of their data so they could make plans for the future.

But the cubes were not perfect. One notable problem with them is that they require someone to translate data from a file or an intermediate relational database and into the cube format. So experienced users should be able to write and master formulas in the MDX language.

Even today, using an OLAP cube requires a considerable amount of information and knowledge on the part of the IT and technology infrastructure expert or consultants with specific OLAP training. For startups or small businesses, the cost of hiring a professional to manage cubes can be prohibitive.

VBA and Macro

A macro is nothing more than a program written in VBA (Visual Basic for Applications), a language that can also be used to make macros or programs in other Microsoft Office applications.

In very general terms, a macro is a sequence of actions that you can execute one or more times as needed.

Excel offers us for the occasion a tool, called a macro recorder, which allows the automatic transformation of all operations performed with mouse and keyboard into a series of instructions contained precisely within a macro, thus allowing us to repeat the entire sequence of operations simply by starting our macro.

Let us imagine, to remain in the field of examples, that we find ourselves in a work situation where it often happens with some frequency that we have to transform the contents of cell ranges containing formulas into their result. In manual terms ni we will select the range of our interest, give the Copy command and then choose the Paste Special command by selecting values as the paste option; then, we will execute the Paste Special command in the same range selected with the Copy command.

Now let us create this process using a macro.

After selecting the range we are interested in, we will go to the View and Macro tab and then, after clicking on Macro, we will execute the record macro command.

At this point the Record Macro window will appear. Here we will enter a name for our macro; it is good practice for the name chosen to reflect the operation of the macro. In the Hotkey box we will type any letter so that when typing from our keyboard the combination CTRL + chosen key our macro will start.

In the Store Macros box we leave the option this workbook as well, alternatively, once you get the hang of it, you can choose the macro-personal folder option thus creating your own personal collection of macros that you can use in your projects. After clicking OK the window will close and from that moment on, whatever commands or operations we go to do in our worksheet, record macro will record them.

When we're done, just select the Macro command from the view tab and select the stop recording command.

At this point our macro will be ready. All we have to do to try it out is to position ourselves on a new range and press the key combination CTRL+ the letter of our choice.

It may happen to you that the first time you try to create a macro the operation is blocked by a security warning that prevents creation in this way. Unfortunately, for more than a few years now, some have begun to spread computer viruses that associate with any computer viruses that are embedded in Office documents.

Opening these documents containing the macro-infects can create a variety of problems, from simple jokes that only create a bit of confusion or annoyance to, unfortunately, real big problems. Microsoft took immediate action by creating macro virus protection that is immediately activated once Excel is installed. So without descending into excessive concern, we always pay a little attention when we receive a document with a macro attached especially if it comes from senders unknown to us.

Instead of recording macros, we might also consider creating them directly by writing VBA statements in the Visual Basic editor.

This would allow us to make one more evolution, since macro-registered macros are not capable of achieving certain results.

For example, in many cases it might be useful to receive user input before or during the execution of a macro, or to need, in the case of a printout, to ensure that rows with a value equal to zero are not printed. Or, again, we may need a macro that handles a particularly complex or nested function (a kind of macro within a macro) that, with the macro registered, would be impossible to have.

In this case we will need to know the Visual Basic for Application programming language.

In summary, what are we talking about? VBA (Visual Basic for Application) is a reprise of a programming language, called BASIC, from which it takes its instructions. The complexity of the language arises from the fact that these instructions can on the one hand refer to variables (numbers or letters), but they can also use Excel objects. Objects, expressed very lightly, are programming constructs that aggregate sets of data and instructions, forming a self-contained whole.

Excel objects can be configured in a very simple way (think rectangles, for example) or decidedly complex (remember pivot tables). The entire workbook, for example is considered an object while Excel cells are not, the cell ranges are, and this is very important to clarify, the cell ranges. Now the objects that we are going to consider have two dimensions that are fundamental: property and method.

If we were to find ourselves in the situation of describing an object familiar to us to a person who does not know it we would use the name of this object (property) and a verb (method). Let us try to rephrase what is written in a more layman's way: a car is considered an object, its properties correspond to make and color while methods are the actions that the car can perform.

This is also true of Excel objects, which themselves have properties that can characterize them even uniquely and methods that are nothing more than the actions these objects can perform or we want them to perform.

Objects deserve their own treatment because they are the cornerstone of what is modern programming referred to as, precisely, object-oriented programming defined by the acronym OOP (Object-Oriented Programming).

In computer terminology, the set of instructions (or vulgarly lines that make up our listing) written in a given programming language is called source code.

VBA is what in computer science terms is called a high-level language. A high-level language means a programming language designed and created so that it can be more easily understood and studied by humans. In fact, commands borrowed from the English language are used in VBA that allow for significantly easier memorization.

The uses of this programming language are vast, we go from creating simple macros for personal use of a simple project we need to much more elaborate constructions for an enterprise level by creating real Excel-based programs that can route or extend its computing and operational power.

If you are intrigued enough, we can take this one step further, always remember well though that this is not a VBA programming book. What you will have in this chapter will be just a simple and immediate first knowledge base of this programming language.

Before we approach the code, and it will be just a first read and example code nothing therefore elaborate or sophisticated, it is important to begin to familiarize ourselves with what are the basics of this programming language which we will now try to see in extreme summary:

Variables: variables are letters, notoriously the most popular ones are used since they are borrowed from mathematical algebra, such as x and y. Writing x=4 assigns a value to the variable. You must imagine the variable as if it were an empty box that must be filled either with a value or even a formula. Remember: filled.

A variable must always be assigned, that is, have a value; it cannot remain empty. Do not abuse variables too much, remember that they have an allocation in memory, that is, they occupy a certain space of the computer's memory.

What name can I choose to identify my variables? Just x and y? Absolutely not, the choice of variable names is free but it behooves you to keep in mind some basic little rules: you must not use basic VBA words to identify your variables.

Basic words in VBA are those words that have special meanings in our programming language and cannot in any way be used to name variables. You cannot use spaces in variable names, if you need to separate names you can alternate between upper and lower case or use the underscore character (_), never, I repeat never, use space.

Finally, as mentioned earlier for other situations in our book, try to use a name that can indicate what our variable contains or why this variable was created. This will help you not only in memorization, but also in reading the code and intervening if there are any errors.

As for arithmetic operators, the same ones as in Excel are used with, again importantly, the same concept of using parentheses. These operators are:

Addition (+);

Subtraction (-);

Multiplication (*);

Division (/).

Same for the logical operators we have already encountered in Excel for conditional choices:

IF

OR

NOT

AND

TRUE

140

Now we need to activate the commands tab inherent in VBA programming contained in Excel, this is because, normally by default, this tab is not activated in Excel. To do this, after creating a new workbook, we go to File, activate the Other item and then Options. Here, within the window we select the Ribbon Customization item and place a check mark on the Development item as shown in Figure 14.1.

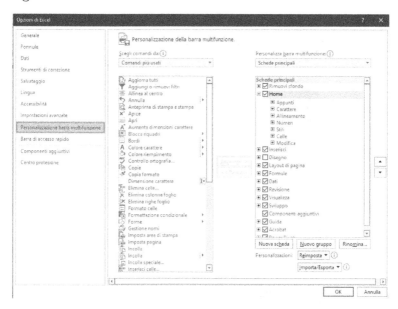

Figure 14.1 Options Window

By pressing the left button of our mouse at the ok button, we could see the Development tab materialized within our ribbon as you can see for yourself in figure 14.2.

Figure 14.2 Development tab

We are now ready to tackle our first program in VBA.

As has been said before, this is not a book on programming in VBA; therefore, we will stop only at a first and simple example, which, as all computer programming books well teach, will be the now famous Hello World.

What we want to do is tickle your curiosity by prompting you to delve into this language, which, beyond the terminologies that may seem somewhat hostile to you, possesses a good learning curve.

Once Excel is open, we select our now-famous Development tab within the ribbon. Here, positioning ourselves at the beginning of our sequence of commands we click on the Visual Basic command allowing us to open the Editor of this programming language. The Editor is nothing more than the window in which we are going to write our source code.

Once our Editor is open we start typing the first instruction which will be Sub Hello (). You will notice two things right away, the first is that the Editor writes immediately below the following instruction End Sub and that both Sub and End are written in blue color.

Sub is the beginning statement of a program in VBA and must always be followed by the name we want to give our program, which in this case is Hello. End Sub, on the other hand, is the end statement of the program written in VBA. Remember that whenever you write a program you must always end it with this instruction.

The blue coloring indicates that both Sub and End Sub are special words and therefore take on that coloring. Remember that special words, typical of VBA, cannot take the name of any variable as mentioned earlier.

Having written these instructions we have a program in VBA that is structurally and syntactically sound, the problem being that it does absolutely nothing. Our goal is to have the program display the Hello World message.

Let us, therefore, add a new statement to our program which will be as follows:

MsgBox "Hello World"

MsgBox stands for MessageBox is already from its full name can make you understand what this instruction is going to do. As we had written before, you can now see the undoubted advantage of a high-level programming language.

Now our program, duly completed, is as follows:

Sub Hello()

MsgBox "Hello World"

End Sub

Now it is time to see the price of our computer effort. In our Editor's bar we click on the icon of a green triangle with the vertex looking to the right (this is the same icon famously used in music players to indicate the play button).

The result, in all its glory, will be a window that plays the message we have inserted within our source code. Figure 14.3 shows the merit of our computer labors.

Translated with www.DeepL.com/Translator (free version)

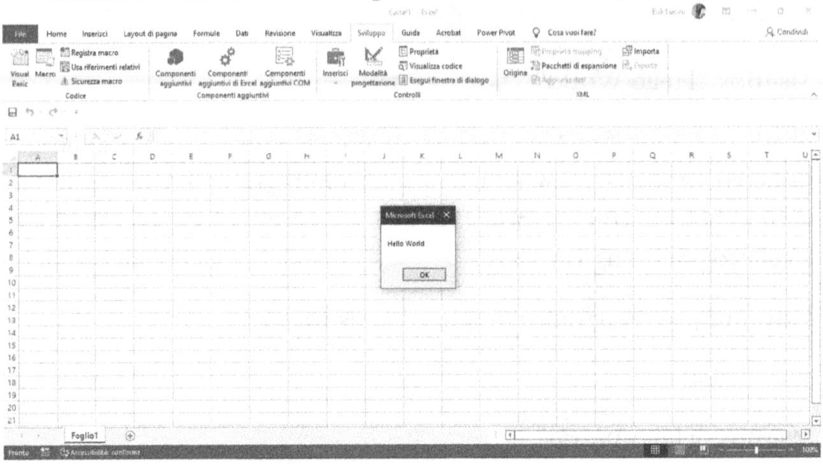

Figure 14.3 Result of the code

You may be wondering why I chose the string "Hello World" instead of "Hello World. There are two simple reasons that pushed me toward this choice: the first is that the Hello World program is the standard, as I have already had occasion to write, of all programming languages.

Any programming course in any language you want will always present to you, as the first example of programming, the Hello World program. In computer science, especially in programming, traditions are built up and handed down. The second is that, like all other level languages, its special words are in English; if you get used to writing the names of variables in this language, you will soon notice that your learning curve of this language, but it is true for a bit of all, will get faster and faster.

It should be added that sentences of any length can be inserted into the source code written in VBA in order to be able to explain and comment on the code. It should be pointed out that commenting on code is an important and useful practice in programming.

144

When we are faced with very long source code listings, comment lines allow us to understand at a first reading what individual blocks of code or the simple line are doing. The important function of such an operation is quickly stated: commenting on the code greatly improves the readability of our program and allows us, should any errors emerge, to immediately trace the affected portion of code or, ultimately, to add a few more options to a function that we had already included in our program.

How can I then comment on the code? To signal comment lines to the syntactic checker (the one that checks our code) in our Editor, we simply start each comment line with an apostrophe. Our Editor will then immediately recognize the comment lines by coloring them green.

One last thing: in our Editor there is also provision for the creation of graphical elements such as buttons and tables whose code will be inserted into our listing. Here, too, always be careful not to overburden your program with too many elements. Buttons, windows should always be chosen wisely.

Contrary to what you might think, you can get oriented fairly quickly in the VBA language to the point of creating even macros that are not particularly demanding.

The advice is to delve into this programming language because it will allow you to calibrate Excel to you like a tailored suit.

Not only that, but you will really touch the full power of this software by contributing, thanks to the macro, to make it even more efficient and complete. By learning to program in VBA you will see that Excel, at some point, will seem to have come to life.

Conclusions

Mastering Excel definitively is not easy; its structure, its way of "thinking," its constructs all require a precision effort that many times slips from our keyboard keys. When we seem to have gotten close, Excel seems to raise the bar some more to challenge us in knowledge.

Power queries, power Pivot, VBA all seem to displace us but draw us in like a kaleidoscope of a thousand colors. The more complete Excel becomes, the more it leaves us feeling that we are not complete.

Excel is a program that demands a lot from us, but in return it facilitates our work by making it fast, precise and now decisive.

Today, knowing Excel means knowing much of work automation, data-driven decision making, value returns or employee performance. Today, this software is becoming the beating heart of administration. Knowing it, mastering it, and expanding it has become fundamental to the new work arrangement.

We do not pretend to have disclosed to you all the doors by leaving this program free of secrets, but what I am most pressed in the writing of this paper is to make you understand how Excel speaks and reasons, what it can do for you and your projects, and to leave you with that hint of curiosity so that, strong in your legs and in the knowledge we have provided, you can become so passionate and curious about it that you will continue the growth of this knowledge on your own. A knowledge that only comes through understanding.

As Albert Einstein said Any fool can know. The point is to understand.

different things. They can assign a value to whatever variable you are working on, they can compare different variables to see if they are alike or different, and they can even do some mathematical equations for you. There is just so much that the operators are going to be able to do to help you out. Some of the different types of operators that you can work with include:

Arithmetic Operators

The arithmetic operators are responsible for helping you to do various mathematical equations. If you need to add a few variables together or do something else similar, these are the ones that you will need to work with. Some of the arithmetic operators that you are able to choose from include:

(+): this is the addition operator.
(-): this is the subtraction operator
(*): this is the multiplication operator
(/): this is the operator for division
(%); this is the modulo operator
(++): this is the increment operator and is used to increase the value of your operand by one.
(--): this is the decrement operator and it is

used in order to decrease your operands value by one.

One thing to remember when working on your code is that you are able to use multiple of these inside of the same part. You can add together more than two numbers or you can do a combination and add together a few numbers before subtracting others and so on. You just need to remember that the order of operations is going to come into play here and the system is going to go in a certain manner in order to get the right answer. It is going to first multiply, and then divide, and then move on to addition and subtraction, going from left to right, to get the correct answer.

Relational operators

Next on the list is the relational operators. These are the ones that will compare whether the two operands you have are equal or not equal and then give you the right result at the end. The most common types of relational operators that you may find include:

(==): this is the equal to operator. If the two values are equal, you will get a true result.

(!-): this operator is the not equal operator.
(>): this is the greater than operator.
(<): this is the less than operator.
(<=): this is less than or equal to.
(>=): this is greater than or equal to.

When you are working on the relational operators, you are working with the Boolean data type. This means that the result you are getting will be either true or false. If the answer gives you a return of true, it means that the statement that is connected to your code is going to be executed. But if it ends up that the statement is false, the code is going to end; if you set up a conditional statement, it will be the second statement that releases if your answer returns a false.

Logical operators

There are several logical operators that you will be able to use inside of your C# code including;

(&&): this is the logical AND. It is only going to show up as true if both of your operands are true.
(||): this is the logical OR. This operator is going to give you true for an answer if at least

one of your operands ends up being true.
(^): this is the logical exclusive OR and it will result in a true if one of your operators is true.
(!): this one will be able to reverse the value of the Boolean variable.

These are similar to the relational operator because it is also going to be seen as a Boolean answer. Your return is going to be either true or false and depending on the conditions that you set up, you will be able to get the right statements to show up on the screen.

Working on Your First Code

Here we will need to open up the compiler for C# and get started on our very first code. Here is what we will need to write out to get that to work:

```
using System;
using System.Collections.Generic;
using SystemLinq;
using System.Text;
using System.Threading.Tasks;

namespace HelloWorld
{
```

```
        //A simple program to display the
words Hello World

        class Program
        {
                static void Main(string[] args)
                {
                        Console.WriteLine("Hello
World!");

                        Console.Read();
                }
        }
}
```

As you work on this code, you may see that while you are typing, there is sometimes a box that appears that will provide you with tips or other help. This is the Intellisense part that comes with the VSC compiler and it is good for beginners who need some help with the code they are writing. If you are uncertain that you are writing the code properly or you don't know what you should write out next, this is a good thing to look for. Once you have this code typed into the compiler, you can push on the Start button on your menu so that the program is executed.

If you have some trouble getting the VSC running, you will see that the compiler will provide you with the "Output Window" error. You will be able to push on the error to see what it is and make the changes that are needed before running the program.

Now, if you wrote the code properly, and the program doesn't bring up any other issues, you should have a little black window that comes up on your screen that says "Hello World" inside. When you see this and are satisfied with the work, you will can exit out of this by pressing the Enter key. And now you are done with the first program you need for C#.

Chapter 3: The C++ Programming Language

The C++ language is another one that you may want to add into the mix when you are learning ow to work with the coding languages. It is simple to learn and you are going to love some of the results that you get. It is a bit easier to learn compared to the C# language and it provides you with many great programs that you are going to love. Before getting started, make sure to visit https://www.microsoft.com/en-us/download/details.aspx?id=5555 to get it ready for your computer. Let's take a look at some of the great things that you are able to do with this coding language.

The Hello World Program

Now that you have had some time to set up your environment, it is time to work on your first code and learn how to write a program in this language. We are going to work on the Hello World code and see how easy it is to write out the first code inside this language. In order to get the screen to print out Hello World, you would need to type in the following:

```
#include <iostream>
using namespace std;

//main() is where program execution begins

int main()
{
        cout <<"Hello World"; //prints Hello World
        return 0;
}
```

Now that we have written out the code, we need to look at all the parts to learn what they mean. First, C++ will involve a variety of headers which are used to hold onto useful information and data for the program. The <iostream> header is the one required for this code. We then moved on to adding in the line "using namespace std". At this area, we are telling the compiler which namespace to bring up your information.

The int main() part is going to tell the program that this is the primary function where the program should start being executed and the two slashes are comments that let other programmers know what you are doing in the code without effecting how well the code works. All of this is going to come together in order to print off "Hello World" onto the screen.

Comments in the Code

Comments are important when working inside of the C++ coding language. These are going to help you to explain certain parts of the code to the other programmers who may be looking through the code or can even be used as a way to name your new code. If you use the right symbols inside of the comment, the compiler is just going to skip right over the comment so any comments that you write out won't mess up the code or change anything.

If you would like to write out a comment inside of your code, you would need to use the /* at the beginning of the code and then the */ at the end of the code to show the compiler that you are done writing out the comment at this point.

C++ Variables

When we are working inside of C++, a variable is going to give you a name for the storage of data inside of the program. Each of the variables that you have inside of the C++ program is going to have a specific type, even with this particular code that you are working on. The variable is going to also work to determine the size as well as the layout of the memory for the variable and the range of values that you can store inside of the memory.

When it comes to naming the variables, you will be able to use the underscore character, digits, and letters in order to get it named right, but you will need to make sure that the beginning is either an underscore or a letter rather than a number. There are many variables that you will be able to use, but the most common types include:

Bool: this is going to store values of false or true.
Char: this is going to usually just be one letter or number and it is considered a type of integer.
Int: this is often considered the natural size of the integer.
Void: this is the one that you will use if there is

an absence of a type in your code.

You will want to declare your variables so that the compiler knows that there is one present and is able to know the type and the name before proceeding. The variable declaration will have meaning only when it is compiled because the compiler will actually need a definition of the variable when it is time to link them up. If you are using several files in order to define the variable, you will need to go through a variable declaration. The extern keyword is the best for helping to declare the variable at any place that you want in the code.

A good example of writing out a variable inside this language includes the following;

```
#include <iostream>
using namespace std;

// Variable declaration:
extern int a, b;
extern int c;
extern float f;

int main () {
  // Variable definition:
```

```
int a, b;
int c;
float f;

// actual initialization
a = 10;
b = 20;
c = a + b;

cout << c << endl ;

f = 70.0/3.0;
cout << f << endl ;

return 0;
}
```

Chapter 4: The Python Programming Language

Python is considered one of the best coding languages if you are a beginner. It is really easy to use and can even be combined with a lot of the other coding languages if you are looking on getting started and want to add in some more power along the way. It is one of the best and has a huge support group to help you out with any of the programs that you want to create. To get the Python language on your computer, visit www.python.org/downloads

There are so many things that you are able to do in order to get a code up and running on Python. Many people may avoid using Python because they think that it is too simple or it just isn't going to get the job done. But in reality, it is simple just for the fact that even a beginner is able to learn how to use it, but that doesn't mean that you aren't able to do a lot with it. This chapter is going to take some time to look at the different commands that you can do with Python programming in order to make your programs and codes come to life.

Variables

Variables may sound like something that is too complicated to learn, but they are basically locations in the memory that are reserved in order to store the values of your code. When you work on creating a variable, you are reserving this spot in the memory. In some cases, the data type that is in the variable will tell the interpreter to save the memory space and can even decide what you are able to store on your reserved memory.

Assigning values to your variables

The value is going to be one of the basic things that your program will need to work with. It can be a string, such as Hi World, 3.14, which is considered a type float, or a whole number like 1, 2, and 3 which is considered an integer. Python variables will not need an explicit declaration in order to reserve the space in the memory that you need. This is something that is going to happen automatically whenever you place a value with the variable. For this to work, simply place the (=) so that the value knows where it is supposed to go.

Some examples of this include:

X = 10   *#an integer assignment*
Pi = 3.14   *#a floating point assignment*
Y= 200   *#an integer assignment*
Empname = "Arun Baruah"   *#a string
assignment*

Keep in mind that when you are working on codes, you are able to leave a comment with your wok by using the # sign. This allows you to explain what is going on in the code, leave some notes, or do something else within the program. It is not going to be read by the interpreter since it is just a little note that you are leaving behind for yourself or for someone else.

The next part is going to depend on which version of Python you are using. Python 2 is fine with you writing out print and then the information you want to talk about but Python 3 is going to require you to place the parenthesis in to make it work. An example would be:

```
Print("y = %d" %y)
Print("x = %d" %x)
```

33

Pring("Employee Name is %s" %empname)

These would then be put through the interpreter and the outputs that you would get should be

X = 10
Y = 200
Employee Name is Arun Baruah

Now go through and put in this information to your program and see what comes up. If you didn't get the right answers like listed above, you should go and check that the work is done. This is a simple way to show what you are able to do with Python and get the answers that you need.

Multiple Assignments

In addition to working with the single variables that were listed above, you will also be able to work on multiple assignments. This means that you are going to be able to assign one value to several different variables at the same time. To do this, you would just need to place the equal sign between all of them to keep things organized and to tell the computer that the value is going to be with all of the variables together. You can keep them separated out if that is easier for you, but using this method is going to help you to send everything to the same memory location on the computer and will give the code a clearer look on your screen.

A good example of how to give more than one variable the same value includes:

```
a = b = c = 1
```

This is telling the code that you want all of them to be tied with the value of 1 and that all of these variables should have the same value and that you want to assign them all to the same location within your memory.

Standard Data Types

Another thing that you are able to work on when doing Python is the various data types. These are going to be used in your code in order to define the operations that you can do on each data type as well as explain to others the storage method that will be used for this kind of data. Python has five data types that are considered standard including:

Numbers
Dictionary
Tuple
List
String
Numbers

Number data types are the ones that will store the numeric values. They are going to be created as objects once you assign a value to them. There are also four different types of numericals that Python will support including

Complex (such as complex numbers)
Float (floating point real values
Long (long integers that can also be shown as hexadecimal and octal.)
Int (signed integers)

One thing to note is that while Python will allow you to use the lowercase l when doing the long form of a number, it is best to go with an uppercase L whenever you are using the letter. This is going to help you avoid confusion in reading the program between the l and the 1 as they look really similar. Any time that Python is displaying a long integer that has the l in it, you will see the uppercase L.

Strings

Strings are identified in Python as a contiguous set of characters that will be shown by the use of quotations marks. Python is going to allow for either double quotes or single quotes, but you do need to keep things organized. This means that if you use a double quote at the beginning of your string, you need to end that same string with the double quote. The same goes when you are using a single quote. Both of these will mean the same thing, you just need to make sure that you are using the proper quote marks to make the code look good and to avoid confusing the Python program.

In addition to being able to print off the string that you would like, you are also able to tell the program to print just part of the string using some special characters. Let's look at some of the examples of what you are able to do with the strings, and the corresponding signs that you will use at well, to help illustrate this point.

```
str = 'Hi Python!'
print(str)      #prints complete string
print(str[0])  #prints the first character of the
string
print(str[2:5])         #prints characters starting
from the 3rd to the 5th
print(str[2:]) #prints string starting from the
3rd character
print(str*2)    #prints the string two times
print(str+"Guys")    #prints concatenated
string
```

For the most part you are probably going to
want to print out the whole string to leave a
message up on your program so the first print
that you do is going to be enough. But if you
just want to print out Hi or some other
variation of the words above, you may find that
the other options are really useful. You can do
any combination of these, they are just
examples to help you get started!

Lists

Lists are one of the most versatile data types

that you can work on in Python. In this language, the list is going to contain different items that are either enclosed with the square brackets or separated out with commas.

They are similar to the arrays that you would see in C if you've worked with that program. The one difference that comes up with these is that the items that are in a list can be from different data types.

The values that are stored inside the list can be accessed with a slice operator as well as the [:} symbol with the indexes starting at 0 at the beginning of the list and then working down until you get to -1. The plus sign will be the concatenation operator while you can use the asterisk as the repetition operator. For some examples of what all this means and how you can use the different signs within your programming, consider some of these examples:

list = ['mainu', 'shainu', 86, 3.14, 50.2]
tinylist = [123, 'arun']
print)list)   #prints complete list
print(list[0]) #prints the first element of the list

print(list[1:3]-   #prints elements starting
from the second element and going to the third
print(list [2:])   #prints all of the elements
of the list starting with the 3rd element.
Print(tinylist*2)   #prints the list twice.
Print(list + tinylist) #prints the concatenated
lists.

Dictionaries

Dictionaries are another kind of tool that you can use when you are working in Python. They are similar to a hash table type and they are going to work similar to the hashes or the arrays that you can find on other programming languages like C# and Perl.

They will also consist of key value pairs and while the key can be almost any type on Python, you will notice that they are usually going to be strings or numbers. For the most part, when it comes to values, you will find that they are an arbitrary object in python.

Some examples of how this will work include the following codes:

#dictionary stores key-value pair, later to be

retrieved by the values with the keys
dict = {}
dict['mainu'] = "This is mainu"
dict[10] = 'This is number 10"
empdict = {'name': 'arun', 'code':23, 'dept': 'IT'}

print(dict['mainu']) #this will print the value
for the 'mainu' key
print(dict[10])   #this will print the
value for the 10 key
print(empdict)   #this will print the
complete dictionary
print(empdict.keys())   #this will print out
all of the keys
print(empdict.values()) #this will print all
the values

One thing to keep in mind is that these dictionary values are not going to be stored in an order that is sorted. They aren't going to have the concept of ordering among the elements. This does not mean that you can say that the elements are out of order, they are just going to be unordered.

Keywords

Most of the types of programming languages that you will deal with will have some keywords or words that are reserved as part of the language. These are words that you really shouldn't use in your code unless you absolutely can't help it.

There are 33 keywords found in the most recent version of Python and you will need to spell them properly if you want them to do the job that you lay out. The 33 keywords that you should watch out for include:

False
Class
Finally
Is
Return
None
Continue
For
Lambda
Try
True
Def
From

Nonlocal
While
And
Del
Global
Not
Yield
As
Elif
If
Or
Assert
Else
Import
Pass
Break
Except
In
Raise

Keep this list on hand if you are worried about learning the language. It will be able to help you out any time that you have issues with the interpreter about the names that you are giving the variable. You may be confused about why it is giving you some issues with the words you chose, you can go through with this list and see if you used one of the keywords inappropriately within your code.

Statements

When you are writing your code in the Python language, you are going to be making expressions and statements to get it done. Expressions are going to be able to process the objects and you will find them embedded within your statements.

A statement is basically a unit of code that will be sent to the interpreter so that it can be executed. There are two types of statements that you can use; assignment so far and print.

You will be able to write out the statement, or multiple statements, using the Python Shell to do so interactively or with the Python script using the .py extension that we talked about later.

When you type these statements into the interactive mode, the interpreter will work to execute it, as long as everything is properly in place, and then you can see the results displayed on the screen. When there are quite a few lines that you need to write in code, it is best to use a script that has a sequence of statements. A good example of this is:

```
#All of these are statements
X = 56
Name = "Mainu"
Z = float(X)
Print(X)
Print(Name)
Print(Z)
```

Operands and operators

There are a lot of great symbols that are going to show up when you make a code in your Python program. It is important to understand what parts you are able to work with and what they are all going to mean. Operators are often used to mean subtraction, addition, division, and multiplication. The values of the operator will be called operands. You can use many different signs for these in order to get the values that you would like to see.

While you are using the operators and operands, you need to remember that there is going to be an order of evaluation that is followed. Think about going back to math class and how this all worked. You had to look for specific signs in order to figure out which tool you were supposed to use in order to come up with the right answer. This is the same when using these operands within your code.

When you have more than one of these operators in the expression, you will need to do the order of evaluation based on the rules of precedence. For anything that is arithmetic, Python is going to use the acronym PEMDAS which is parenthesis, exponentiation, multiplication, division, addition, and subtraction. If there are a number of these that are the same, such as two sets of numbers that need to be multiplied together, you will need to work from left to right to get the correct number.

Another important operator that you should look for is the modulus operator. This one is going to work with integers and is going to yield the remainder once the first operand has been divided by the second one.

Chapter 5: Working with the C Coding Language

Working with the C language is pretty simple. You can write a code that just has one line or you can go on and write a nice long one that is going to be more complex and could run a game or some other process. While you can get more complex later on, I am going to look at some of the basics of writing inside of the C language to help you to get comfortable. A good place to start when looking for downloading the C language (and to get Visual Studio with it which is one of the best), includes:
https://www.visualstudio.com/vs/

Writing a Dummy Code

First, let's take a look at writing out your dummy code. This isn't going to bring you an output like some of the other codes that we will discuss later on, but it will help you to get the hang of creating and saving a code in the C language so you are ready for the things we do later on.

So to start, you need to go into the Code Blocks IDE, or whichever IDE that you chose, and click on the New Button. You will want to open up an Empty File. Now you will need to type in a code into the editor so that you are able to create a code to save. I am going to keep this simple and just type in one line like the following:

```
main() {}
```

Now you will need to save the source file and you can do this by clicking on the Save button. You can either let this save on the default of your computer or you can choose the folder that you would like all of these code files to be saved on your computer; the choice is up to you, just remember where you are saving all of these so if you need to find them later.

Make sure to name the file something that you will be able to remember later on, or you will get confused as you start to add on more of these files over time. I am going to call this file "dummy.c". Once you have saved this, the source code file is created and it has been saved on your computer. Now you will click on the Build button.

You will notice that the code is not going to compile. What you are going to see is the minimum of the C program, which is also called the dummy. All of your codes in C need to have the main function because this is where the execution of the program is going to start; you will just need to put the main function inside of the curly brackets.

Since this is a dummy source code and one where we are just experimenting a little bit, I didn't have us put any code into the curly brackets. When you try to run this option, you will not get an output because nothing was placed inside. We will be able to add in different things later on and create an output based on what is inside the code. You may see a compiler warning when entering the dummy code, but this is not critical. You will just click on your Run button and then find that it is not able to give you any output.

Congratulations! You have just written your very first code using the C programming language. If you didn't get any output, you did the code right. This is just the basic form of writing a code in the C language and there is so much more that you are able to add into the code. Some of the other basic parts that you can add into your code includes:

Structure
Variables and values
Operators
Functions
Keywords

I am going to take you through how some of these work so you can learn how to make the code shine the way that you would like.

Writing Another Code

Now that I have had some time to explain a few of the basic parts of code writing, let's take a look at how this would work by bringing out our dummy.c program from earlier. Just open up the code from wherever you stored it before and I am going to make the main function be defined as an integer function. This basically means that it is going to return an integer value onto the operating system. We will need to do some editing in order to make this happen.

Inside of your editor, you will need to add in the keyword "int" before your "main" part to ensure that you are getting the integer output that you would like. Make sure that you place a space between both of these keywords to help the compiler to read through both of them. So to start, type out the following code:

```
int main()
{
}
```

You will notice that the code is a bit different than we originally wrote out with the first code, but putting the curly brackets in this manner is what most veteran programmers prefer to use. Now it is time to add in a statement to this main function so that it will actually show you an output. I will keep it simple and just add in the number three.

You will first need to type in the "return" and then the number three. I will write out the example of the syntax that you would use to make this happen:

```
int main()
{
        return(3);
}
```

Make sure to add in the semicolon after the statement. Save the file and then click on the Build button. As long as you type in the code like I wrote above, you shouldn't have any issues with errors or messages coming up for you. Click on the Run Button.

When using a Linux or Mac system, it is possible that you won't see any output other than the build log, and it will say that the program terminated with a status of zero. On a PC computer, the terminal window is going to show you the return value 3.

Any time that you want to add in an output to your dummy program, you need to bring in the output function. The keywords in the C language aren't going to output anything because they are just basic vocabulary, such as the words int and return. You can do this by using the "puts" command inside the program.

Let's take a look at how this is going to work when you write out some code. Make sure that the function of the "puts" is inside of parenthesis and that you place in a string of text between a double quote to make it work properly. Here is the example I am going to use:

```
int main()
{
        puts("I am the King of the C
programming world");
                return 3;
}
```

When you save this source code and then click on Build, you should see a warning come up on your computer. Even if you don't see this, you need to realize that you have another step to do at this point. Before the puts function is going to work, it needs to have a definition inside, or you will find that the compiler is confused. The definition of your puts will be in the I/O header file and you need to place this into the source code with the help of the preprocessor directive.

Here is an example of how that would look inside of your code to keep things organized and to avoid errors.

```
#include<stdio.h>
```

```
int main()
{
        puts("I am the King of the C
programming world");
                return 3;
}
```

This version includes the preprocessor directive
along with the definition for the puts function.
You can save the file and then click on the Build
and Run buttons that are at the top of the
editor. If everything is typed properly, you can
avoid errors and in the output terminal
window, the statement that you wrote out for
the puts function as well as the value 3 will
show up on the screen.

Learning some of the basics of writing a code in
the C language can make it easier to understand
what is going on. I showed you a few of the
options that you have when working inside of
the C language, but there is still so much more
that you are able to do. Take some time to get
familiar with how these codes work, play
around with the IDE and the compiler, and get
comfortable before moving on and learning
some more complex options when writing your
own code.

Chapter 6: The JavaScript Programming Language

JavaScript is a good coding language to learn if you want to work on a website or online. This one often goes with the Java program, remember that these two are separate, in order to add some little add-ins into the whole program. It is really easy to learn and can make all the difference in how your program is going to work. Let's take a look at how the JavaScript program will work as you first get started.

Getting Started on JavaScript

The first thing we will need to do here is download the JavaScript language by visiting www.javascriptlint.com/download.htm. JavaScript is a versatile coding language that you are able to inject anywhere you would like in your page. As long as you have the HTML tags <script>...</script> around what you would like to insert. But in most cases, you will be recommended to place the script that you want to use in between the head sections or the <head>...</head> tags.

When the browser is taking a look at the content on the page, or the HTML on the page, it is going to just read through the whole thing like reading through a book. But when the browser program comes to the <script> tag, it will start to interpret whatever you have written between these tags and won't stop until it reaches the </script> part of the tag. This allows the program to interpret what you would like to have on the page in any location that you would like.

When working with the script tag, you will be able to give them one of two attributes including:

Language—this is the attribute that will specify what kind of scripting language you are using. The value for the JavaScript language is basically "javascript." If you are using a newer version of HTML, this is something that been phased out so you may not have to worry about it at all.

Type—this is the attribute that will indicate the scripting language that you are using and the value that you are using with it will be set to text/javascript when in the JavaScript language.

Writing a program

At this point you may be a bit confused on what is going on and what all of these things mean. Let's take a chance to open up the html file (use the steps that were in the first chapter if you don't already have this opened up) and then we can get started at writing your first JavaScript program. To do this, just use the code that is below:

```
<!DOCTYPE html>
<html>
<head>
<meta charset- "ISO-8859-1">
<title> My First JavaScript Program </title>
</head>
<body>
        <script language = "javascript"
type = "text/javascript">
        document.write("Welcome to
JavaScript First Program");
        </script>
</body>
</html>
```

This may seem like a lot of information to put into the code, but it is going to ensure that you are getting everything in that is needed to make a great code that others can read through. Let's separate each of the parts out to help you understand what is going on a bit better!

Explaining the code

In this code, the JavaScript code was inserted between the <body> ... </body> tags in the HTML. The code was first declared with the right attributes and then with using the document object you were able to write out the message that helped to welcome others on to the webpage. So when this is executed, the webpage should have the words "Welcome t JavaScript First Program" right at the top.

Output

When you take the HTML program that we just wrote up and try to execute it, the results that you will get would be:

Welcome to JavaScript First Program.

This is basically what you told the computer

system to write so if you have put everything into their right spaces within the code that you were writing, this is the exact phrase that should show up when you are working on the code.

Line breaks and white spaces

When it comes to having spaces in your code, or even line breaks, you can use them as much as you would like. These can often help to clear up what you are writing and you won't have to worry about the code getting too long or too hard to read. That being said, it really doesn't matter how much, if any, space that you put into the code. The browser parser is not going to read these spaces so you can write out the code in the way that works for you.

This makes it easy for you to create the indentation, lines, and other parts that you need in order to make sense of the program, to help format it properly, and to keep it looking nice. Just because the lines and the spaces aren't recognized in JavaScript does not mean that you should completely ignore them in the process.

When you are first getting started with this language, it may be a good idea to add in a few more line breaks and indents to your code. This is going to make it a bit easier to read through and you can catch some of the mistakes a bit easier. The extra white spaces aren't going to change how the system will read through the information, but it can make it easier for you to read the code and for other beginners to know what you are trying to write out.

Using semicolons

For the most part, you will end all of your statements using the semi-colon when you are in JavaScript. These are optional if you are placing the statements on different lines from each other so the choice is really up to you. If you just write out the code with everything on one line as a continuous string, you will need to add in the semicolon but if you are separating out the statements as you go onto different lines, it is your choices whether you would like to use them. It is considered good programming practice to have them there regardless, but the program will work whether you place them there or not. The codes that we have in this guidebook will use the semicolons to help keep things clear.

Case sensitivity

You will notice that JavaScript is one of the languages that is sensitive to the cases that you are using. This means that you need to keep your use of uppercase and lowercase letters consistent throughout the program. This is true for everything that you label including identifiers, function names, variables, and keywords. For example, when you are using JavaScript, LEARN and learn will be different when the programming language is going through it.

This is important to remember when you are naming your functions and statements. If you name one of them JAVASCRIPT and then try to search for it or bring it back out by using the JavaScript word, you are going to get an error sign. You do get some say in what you name them, but try to keep all of the names for the code consistent so that you name them the same way and can easily call them back up when they are needed.

Writing comments

There are times when you will need to write out a comment in JavaScript. You may want to tell someone else a bit more about the program or you are interested in explaining what should be placed in each of the statements. There are a few comment styles that are followed when you are using JavaScript in your coding including:

Single lines—if your comment is just going to take over one line, you simply need to use the double slash (//) to get it started.

Multiple lines—sometimes your comments will be a bit longer and they can take over a few lines. For this you will use /* to start the comment and then */. You are able to use this on single line options as well if you are worried about formatting.

JavaScript will also recognize the HTML comment if you would like to stick with this. The HTML comment is <!--. This will be treated just like a single line comment in this language.

Closing sequence—the HTML closing sequence sign of → is not going to be recognized in JavaScript. If you would like to use this sign in your code, you will need to write it like this: //→.

When you use these options, you are telling the interpreter that it should not read the comment. You are able to put as many of these within your code as you need as long as you use the proper formatting so that the interpreter knows what you are leaving there for others and what it should leave alone. Once the comment is over, the interpreter will go back and start executing whatever else you have written in the code.

There are a lot of different times when you will need to write out a comment to help make sense of things in your code. If you want to tell someone what you are doing within the code, answer some questions, or help yourself or another coder to understand what information needs to go into the statements, these comments are great. You can add in as many of the comments as you would like, as long as you use the right signals, because the compiler will not read through them and won't try to execute them at all.

Some examples of using comments in JavaScript includes:

```
<!DOCTYPE html>
<html>
<head>
<meta charset = "ISO-8859-1">
<title>JavaScript Comments</title>
</head>
<body>
        <script type = "text/javascript">
        <!—The opening sequence single line
comment.
                The closing sequence HTML
comment//-->

        // This is a single line comment.
        /*
 *This is a multiple line comment in JavaScript
*/
        </script>
</body>
</html>
```

Output

When you do the program in HTML that we listed above, the output will just be blank. This is because the whole program is listed out as a comment and the interpreter is not going to lists out the comments because it has learned to not read them after the signals that we discussed above. If you had added in some other code in there, the interpreter is only going to read that and will ignore the comments that you add into the code. You are allowed to put in as many comments as you would like, as you can see from the example above, as long as you choose the right symbols to go with it so that the interpreter does not give you an error sign.

These are just some of the basic things that you need to understand in order to get started with using JavaScript on your own. Each part can help you to write out the syntax that you want and ensures that you are getting the very most out of your written code. Take some time to experiment with the comments and some of the other aspects we have discussed to figure out how these are going to work for you.

Chapter 7: Working with the Java Coding Language

While JavaScript is great at putting some of the add-ins into a website, the Java code is going to be much better for writing up the whole website or other applications that you want to use online. If you are looking to create your own personal or business website, you will want to learn how to work with the Java code. Let's take a look at some of the basics that come with this coding language and how to get started.

Writing out your code in Java

The first step that you will need to do is to download the Java coding language. You can do this by visiting https://java.com/download. Writing code can be simple inside of Java, you just need to get some experience with working inside of the system and with your text editor. To get started with your first code inside of Java, take the following steps.

Step1: to start writing a program in Java, you will first need to set up your work environment. Open up NetBeans or whichever environment you chose for working in Java and get it ready to use.

Step 2: once the environment is up, open up your text editor that you want to use. Notepad is a good selection if you have a Windows computer, but anything that is similar will work out great.

Now we are going to create the Hello World program. This is an easy program to use on any programming language that you want to work with because you will get the hang of how the syntax works and you will get the words "Hello World" to show up on your screen.

To start this, just go to your text editor, click on new file, and then save this document as "HelloWorld.java". HelloWorld is going to be the name of your class, so keep this in mind since the class name needs to be the same as the file name.

One the file is created, it is time to declare the class and the main method. The main method will be the same in terms of method declaration no matter what kind of program you are creating inside of your Java program. At this point, you should have the following syntax:

```
public class HelloWorld {
        public static void main(String[] args) {
        }
}
```

Write this part out into your text editor. Next, you will need to write out the part of the code that will tell your text editor what you would like to have printed out. For this point, you would need to type out:
System.out.println("Hello World.");
This is going to tell the system that you want to print out the phrase "Hello World" onto the screen. You can try this out and change up the message you want to use inside of the program based on what you want to program to use.
With this part, there are a few things that help to make it get done the proper way so let's take a look at how these work.
System: this part is going to alert the system that it needs to do something.
Out: this is going to tell the system that you are creating an output that you want it to print on the screen.
Println: this part will stand for print line in the system. You are basically telling the system that you want to print out the statement that comes after this part.
Parentheses: there are some parentheses that are found around the "Hello World" part. These means that the code in front of it is takin gin a parameter, or the string of Hello World.
So basically this code is working to alert the

system that you need it to take some actions, that you want to create an output and that you want to print out the line "Hello World" onto your screen.

Before continuing, there are a few rules that you should follow when making these codes inside of Java. First, it is a good idea to add a semicolon at the end of the lines. This is a good programming practice and helps the text editor to print things off properly. Java is also a case sensitive language so pay attention to whether you are using upper case or lower case letters when you are writing out class names, variable names, and method names. And finally, any blocks of code that are specific to a certain loop or method will be encased with the curly brackets.

So let's put this code all together so you can place it into your text editor in the right places.

```
public class HelloWorld {
        public static void main(String[] args) {
                System.out.println("Hello
World.");
        }
}
```

Once this is written into the code, it is time to save your files and then open up a command prompt, also known as a terminal, in order to compile the program. You can navigate to the folder where the HelloWorld.java is located. Type in the words javacHellWorld.java. This is going to tell your compiler that you want to compile your HelloWorld.java.

If there happen to beany errors in your code, the compiler will be able to tell you what may be wrong with your code. Otherwise, the compiler is not going to show any messages. You can then look at the directory where you store the HelloWorld.java and inside should be the HelloWorld class that we designed. This is the file that is used when you want to run your program.

Now that we have written a program, you may want to give it a try and see if this will run. Open up the terminal or the command prompt and type out java HelloWorld. This is going to tell Java that you wish to run your HelloWorld class. If everything has gone into the program properly, the statement "Hello World" will show up on the console and you have written your first code in Java!

Expanding the Hello World Program

Working with the Hello World program was pretty simple and has given you some experience with how this program is going to work. Here we are going to take the Hello

World program and extend it out a bit. In the Hello World program, we printed out a string for the user to see, but now we are going to extend out the program so that the users are able to place in their name and then it will greet them by name.

First, we will import in the scanner class. In Java, there are a few libraries that you can access, but you first need to import them. One of the libraries that we need and which holds the Scanner object is the java.util. To import this Scanner class, use the following code:

import java.util.Scanner;

This tells the program that you wish to use your Scanner object, which is inside the java.util package. Inside of the method, we will instantiate a new instance with this Scanner object. To use this Scanner class, we just need to create a new Scanner object that we are able to populate and use the methods of. To get these Scanner objects to work for us, we would need to use the following code:

Scanner userInputScanner = new Scanner(System.in);

So what does this code mean and what is it going to tell the computer to do? Here is an explanation of how the different parts move: userInputScanner: this is the name of the

Scanner object we are using. Note that this is written in what is known as the camel case; which is the conventional way of writing out your variables in Java.

the new operator will help to create a brand new instance of your object. For this instance, we created a new instance in the Scanner object with the new Scanner(System.in) part.

This new Scanner object is going to take in a parameter that will tell the object what they need scanned. The System.in is going to work for this and it tells the program that you want to scan in the input from the system, which is basically going to be the name of the user.

Now we can work on prompting the user for their input. We need to ask the user for the input so that the user has an idea that they are supposed to type something into their console. Otherwise, the program will just sit still because nothing is entered. You can accomplish this with the following code:

System.out.print("What's your name?");

The next part that you should do is ask the scanner object to take in the information that the user types and then have it store that information as a new variable. The Scanner is responsible for taking in the data that your user is typing, which should be their name at this

point. To do this, use the following code:
String userInputName =
userInputScanner.nextLine();
This should tell the Scanner object that you want it to read what the user inputs into the system and use that as the variable for your next part. It can now be used as the greeting that shows back to the user. Since you have the name of the user, you can write it out so that the program mentions the name while leaving another message. The next step is to write out the following code:
System.out.println("hello" + userInputName + "!");
At this point, we have been separating out the code to the different steps and discussing it, but let's put it all together to help you see how this code should be written out:

```
import java.util.Scanner;
public class HelloWorld (
        public static void main(String[] args) {
                Scanner userInputScanner = new
Scanner(System.in);
                System.out.print("What's your
name?");
                String userInputName =
userInputScanner.nextLine():
                System.out.println("Hello" +
```

userInputName + "!");

Once this code is in the system, you will be able to compile the program and run it. Go into your command prompt or the terminal window and then run the same commands that we did with the HelloWorld.java from the last section. You can compile this program by typing in javac HellWorld.java.

When you type in the HellowWorld.java, your program should ask "What's your Name?" You can go through and type in your name. Let's type in the name Jane. Once you press enter on this name, the program will print out Hello Jane and then the program is done.

While this part may take a few more lines to complete, it is still pretty basic. It took the original skills you learned with your first part and expanded it out into a code that has a few extra parts that come with it. Despite needing a few more parts, you will find that this is a basic code that adds in a bit more personalization to the codes you make.

And now you are set to start with the Java program. You already know how to do two basic codes inside of this program and as you move through the other parts, you will be able to write out some more codes to get the hang of

how the text editors work inside this program.
(How To Write Your First JavaScript)

Conclusion

When it comes to working on some coding languages, you will find that there are so many that you are able to choose from. You may worry that it is going to be too hard to get started on a coding language that you will never be able to figure them out, but most of them are pretty easy, you just need to find the place where you are going to get started and then go from there.

This guidebook took some time to explore some of the different programming languages and how you would be able to write some of your first codes inside of them. There are quite a few computer programming languages that you are able to work with, but we took on some of the ones that are the most popular, including Python, Java, JavaScript, C# and C++. These are the ones that are the most widely used and can help you to work on so many different programs that you will be off to a great start in no time.

When you are ready to learn a bit about some of the great computer programming that you have always wanted, it is time to take a look through this guidebook and learn everything that you need about all the best coding languages!

www.ingramcontent.com/pod-product-compliance
Lightning Source LLC
Chambersburg PA
CBHW071306050326
40690CB00011B/2548